KU-448-692

SEIZE THE DAY

with Dietrich Bonhoeffer

CHARLES RINGMA
SEIZE
THE DAY
with Dietrich Bonhoeffer

AN ALBATROSS BOOK

Published in Australia and New Zealand by
Albatross Books Pty Ltd
PO Box 320, Sutherland
NSW 2232, Australia
and in the United Kingdom by
Lion Publishing plc
Peter's Way, Sandy Lane West
Littlemore, Oxford OX4 5HG, England

First edition 1991

National Library of Australia
Cataloguing-in-Publication data

Seize the day with Dietrich Bonhoeffer

ISBN 0 86760 094 2 (Albatross)
ISBN 0 7459 1706 2 (Lion)

1. Meditations. I. Bonhoeffer, Dietrich, 1906–1945. II. Title

242.2

Cover and interior illustrations: Michael Mucci
Printed by Kyodo Printing Co. Pte Ltd, Singapore

CONTENTS

PREFACE
A BRIEF INTRODUCTION
TO BONHOEFFER

January
February
March
April
May
June
July
August
September
October
November
December

APPENDIX
BIBLIOGRAPHY

Dedication

These meditations are selected in the hope that
a new generation of Christians will be inspired to live
the Christian life with a profound spirituality,
a radical obedience and a relevance that
takes seriously the challenge of their era.
In this, they cannot but be inspired by
Dietrich Bonhoeffer.

PREFACE

These meditations from the writings of Dietrich Bonhoeffer are disturbing rather than helpful and 'worldly' rather than pious. Bonhoeffer combined biblical spirituality with political relevance, faith with obedience, peace with resistance, community with rugged individualism and prayer with activism.

While Bonhoeffer's writings are scholarly, he is more a pastoral theologian than a systematic writer: his writings, therefore, are pregnant with relevance for all who grapple with life's meaning and purpose.

These meditations, in the form of one reading for each day of the year, capture many of the important insights scattered throughout Bonhoeffer's writings. One excerpt is quoted at the beginning of each daily devotional. It is accompanied by my reflections, an appropriate Bible reading and a prayer, meditation or thought. I hope they encourage you to read more of Bonhoeffer and to live a life that combines spirituality with a concern for the world and the welfare of your neighbour.

Bonhoeffer uses sexist language. He constantly speaks of 'man' when he is clearly referring to all persons. For example, the statement 'Christ. . . is the truth spoken in the concrete moment, the address which puts a man [sic] in the truth before God' obviously includes Christ's address and challenge to *women*. We have decided not to rewrite Bonhoeffer's use of language, but ask the reader to make the necessary adjustments. In this and in other ways Bonhoeffer was a person of his time, but this should not detract from the value that he holds for our generation.

My affectionate thanks to my wife Rita who has encouraged me to express my long-standing interest in Bonhoeffer by writing this devotional. I owe a great debt, too, to Evert Ringma and Antje Ringma-DeJong, and to Wouter Dijk and Harmina Dijk-Pesman. Also a big thankyou to Desley Jeanneret and Annette Ganter who have skilfully and patiently completed the typing from handwritten notes.

A further thanks to Albatross Books for their willingness to publish. And finally, my appreciation to Professor Dr Klaas Runia who, during a course on Christian Ethics, first placed Bonhoeffer's *The Cost of Discipleship* in my hands.

Charles Ringma
Brisbane, Australia, 1990

A BRIEF INTRODUCTION
TO BONHOEFFER

Bonhoeffer is a controversial figure. He cuts a paradoxical pose and is difficult to put into a particular religious 'box'. Though he is not always easy to understand, he was, without doubt, a person of firm commitment and practical resolve. That he sought to order his life on the words of Jesus of Nazareth is unquestionable. That his commitment led to his own death is a fact.

Bonhoeffer was the product of an upper middle-class family with the usual emphasis on comfort and security, yet he was to plunge himself into the radical insecurity of a discipleship that took the words of Jesus seriously. This was to lead him from the hallowed halls of the University of Berlin, where he taught theology, to active opposition to the Nazi regime. This opposition led him to teach at an illegal seminary of the Confessing Church in Germany. It also eventually led to his becoming involved in counter-espionage activities. For this he was hanged on April 9, 1945.

Bonhoeffer had strong convictions: he could not be contained by others' expectations, for he had heard the voice of his Master. Thus he departed from the family tradition to study theology. Trained in Berlin's liberal scholarly tradition, he embraced the new theology of Karl Barth without becoming his follower. At a time of powerful German national resurgence, with its narrow ideas of *Volk* and racial superiority, Bonhoeffer actively promoted the opposite — a strong ecumenical perspective.

When the Lutheran Church began to yield to the power of the Hitler rhetoric, Bonhoeffer, in 1933, attacked Hitler by rejecting the leadership principle. When the church emphasised structure, Bonhoeffer was living out the reality of community. While the church dreamed about separation, Bonhoeffer was involved in active engagement of the world.

Bonhoeffer can best be understood by locating him in three distinct yet interrelated phases of his life. (For some more specific details of

Bonhoeffer's life, see *APPENDIX: A brief chronology of Bonhoeffer's life.*)

The first phase was that of the Berlin theological scholar. This was the more academic period of Bonhoeffer's life where he sought to bring together the value of his liberal heritage with that of a renewed interest in the Bible. Here Harnack, Barth, Weber, Nietzsche, Gandhi and Luther all mingle together. During this period, Bonhoeffer produced *Sanctorum Communio, Act and Being* and *Christology.*

The second phase saw Bonhoeffer as a leader in the struggle of the Confessing Church's opposition to Hitler's attempt to control the church. He ran an illegal seminary at Finkenwalde, encouraged the Confessing Church's stand on ecumenical, pastoral and political issues, and helped to mould a new generation of young pastors. At this time, he produced his famous *The Cost of Discipleship* and *Life Together*, as well as important papers for the ecumenical movement.

The last phase saw Bonhoeffer move from a failing Confessing Church to an active involvement in the resistance movement within Germany to Hitler. Here he wrestled with the question of God's action in the world outside the precincts of the church. During this period, he wrote his *Ethics*. After his arrest in 1943, his correspondence from prison with his friend Eberhard Bethge was posthumously published as *Letters and Papers from Prison*. (For the complete list of Bonhoeffer's writings, see *BIBLIOGRAPHY*.)

Bonhoeffer thus moves from scholar to pastor to political activist. Yet this movement has a common theme and, in this sense, the three periods of Bonhoeffer's life are interrelated. This common theme is a costly discipleship which calls the follower of Jesus to a life which leaves the safety of the sanctuary to engage a troubled world.

Bonhoeffer believed that our troubled world could be transformed by a believing church. But he held that this could only be possible when the church itself was transformed into the likeness of Christ. Thus faith and commitment, costly action and worldly concern run as a theme throughout Bonhoeffer's life. And from his struggles, faith, prayers, theology, activism, sense of responsibility, vision of the church and willingness to walk the lonely road of obedience, we cannot but be enriched.

January

If they follow Jesus, men escape from the hard yoke of their own laws and submit to the kindly yoke of Jesus Christ.

The hard way is easy

'If they follow Jesus, men escape from the hard yoke of their own laws and submit to the kindly yoke of Jesus Christ.'

The Cost of Discipleship

We long for freedom, but create oppression. We strive for ease, but make it hard for ourselves. We seek to make our own way, yet become lost in the process. We run from God, but create our own idolatry. Therefore, we need to surrender to Christ to find peace. We need to embrace God's words and ways in order to find true liberty. We need to walk the narrow way of obedience to find true fulfilment.

MEDITATION: *Make me a captive, Lord, and then I shall be free.*

Life is more than its circumstances

'The important thing is to make the best use of one's possessions and capabilities — there are still plenty left — and to accept the limits of the situation, by which I mean not giving way to feelings of resentment and discontent.'

Letters and Papers from Prison

We seldom live in ideal circumstances. More often than not, these are less desirable than what we would like them to be. But circumstances need not control the quality of our life. It is what we make of those circumstances that will determine life's direction. It is when we do not give way to fear, anger, disappointment and frustration that we can transcend the limits of our situation.

PRAYER: *Lord, grant that I may live in response to your will and enabling, rather than by my circumstances and weaknesses. Amen.*

Do to others

'When God was merciful to us, we learned to be merciful with our brethren. When we received forgiveness instead of judgment, we, too, were made ready to forgive our brethren. What God did to us, we then owed to others.'

Life Together

The challenge of the Christian life is to act towards others in ways that are similar to the way that God has acted towards us. Since God's attitude towards us is marked by generosity, faithfulness and grace, we cannot but extend a similar quality of response to others. Forgiven we can forgive others, blessed we can enrich others, and set free we can serve others.

PRAYER: *Lord, having freely received from you, help me to bless others with your blessing. Amen.*

Christ: the man for others

'Christ can never be thought of in his being in himself, but only in his relationship to me.'

Christology

Friendship is not so much a matter of plumbing the depths of another person's inner personality. It is rather the growth of security and trust that is born of availability, concern and care. Similarly, we don't know Jesus in the mystery of his person, but more clearly in the light of his actions towards us. Those actions remind us that he is for us in our weakness, struggles and efforts when we seek to serve God, but against us in our pride, self-sufficiency and attempts to place our concerns at the centre of our life.

MEDITATION: *Actions reveal the mystery of our being.*

Table fellowship

'Perhaps the reason why we attach so much importance to sitting down to table together is that table
fellowship is one of the realities of the kingdom of
God.'

Letters and Papers from Prison

An open home flows from an open heart and
hospitality is the joyous sharing of ourselves
and our home as an expression of God's bountiful goodness to us. In that kind of celebration,
eating together reminds us of our need to be
sustained, of our dependence on God as the
gracious provider of the things we need, and of
the joy of fellowship and companionship.

THOUGHT: *As we sit at table, may our eyes also be
opened to see what you, O Lord, have given us in
each other.*

When only prayer will do

'And above all, we must not neglect the greatest service that is left to us, our faithful daily intercession.'

The Way to Freedom

There is much that we can and should do for each other: encourage, challenge, support and serve. But we cannot and should not do everything for others. This will only breed dependence. What we can always do, however, is to pray that God will bring hope, help, grace and courage to those for whom we share concern.

THOUGHT: *The greatest act of friendship is to faithfully pray for those we care about.*

In the world

'Jesus Christ lived in the midst of his enemies. At the end, all his disciples deserted him. On the cross he was utterly alone, surrounded by evildoers and mockers. For this cause he had come, to bring peace to the enemies of God. So the Christian, too, belongs not in the seclusion of a cloistered life, but in the thick of foes.'

Life Together

God has placed us in the midst of life and it is there that we are to work, learn, fellowship, marry, witness and care. Church should strengthen us for our work in the world. Church is not the true fellowship of Christ if it draws us from the world to live for ourselves. Rather it should empower us to live boldly in the midst of the world with all its needs and challenges.

THOUGHT: *Christ was never a recluse. Even though he had such an important mission, he entered life fully and boldly. As his followers we can do no less.*

Being and giving

'What we are in ourselves, and what we owe to others, makes us a complete whole.'

Letters and Papers from Prison

True life means that we should not be selfish or self-effacing. We cannot just live for ourselves, and we cannot live for others in such a way that we lose our own identity and direction. True life has to express itself in a self-assertion that is a free response of gratitude to God and which seeks the well-being of the other.

THOUGHT: *If I withhold myself from the joy of giving, I will shrivel and die; if I lose myself in giving to others, I will abandon myself to extinction; and if I give while I am also a recipient, I will continue to live and give.*

An open ear

'The first service that one owes to others in the fellowship consists in listening to them. Just as love of God begins with listening to his word, so the beginning of love for the brethren is learning to listen to them.'

Life Together

We are often not good listeners because we are preoccupied with our own thoughts and concerns. To serve another person does not mean doing for them what we want, but what they genuinely need. Careful listening to another's hopes, fears and concerns begins to open to us what those needs might be. Our serving which results from careful listening will always be more effective.

THOUGHT: *Careful listening allows us to enter the world of another person. This must always be for the other's benefit, not for our own curiosity.*

Cheap grace

'Cheap grace is the preaching of forgiveness without requiring repentance, baptism without church discipline, communion without confession, absolution without personal confession. Cheap grace is grace without discipleship, grace without the cross, grace without Jesus Christ — living and incarnate.'

The Cost of Discipleship

God's gift of new life in Jesus Christ is not a right that we can claim. It is a gift that we may receive. Christ's gift of life came at the cost of death. The maintenance of that new life does not come easily and cheaply either. It comes as we continue to respond in faith, trust, humility, confession and surrender to Christ as Lord of all of our life.

PRAYER: *Lord, grant that I may not cheapen your grace by receiving it lightly. Rather, may each touch of your goodness make me a better person more dedicated to doing your will. Amen.*

Facing the challenges of life

'I am sure we must rise to the great responsibilities
which are peculiarly our own, and yet at the same
time fulfil the commonplace tasks of daily life.'

Letters and Papers from Prison

Life has its great challenges. It also has its almost mundane responsibilities. It has its creative possibilities and its routine maintenance
structures. Each is equally important. We cannot serve God to the neglect of our families or
give copious time to intercessory prayer while
we fail to relate to the neighbour and neglect to
pay our bills. In doing both the great and the
small, we need to serve God and others.

PRAYER: *Lord, help me to see the small and mundane as worthy of my commitment to you. Amen.*

The 'radical' Jesus

'For the working-class world, Christ seems to be settled with the church and bourgeois society.'

Christology

The Jesus portrayed in the Gospels was neither a middle-class conservative nor a political radical. He did not join the Sadducees or the Zealots. Jesus instead paved the way for a creative alternative to these two positions. His way placed God's concerns at the centre of his activity and rejected the man-made rules which encouraged religiosity, but did not free people from their sin, hopelessness and social rejection. Clearly, Jesus does not belong first of all to the church but to the world, and certainly not to those who have it all, but to those who hunger for justice and mercy.

THOUGHT: *Jesus does not belong to the religious establishment, but to those who seek him in their need.*

My true self

'I often ask myself who I really am. Am I the man
who keeps squirming under these ghastly experiences in abysmal misery? Or am I the man who keeps
scourging himself and outwardly pretends to
others (and to himself as well) that he is a con-
tented, cheerful, easy-going fellow and allows
everyone to admire him for it?'

Letters and Papers from Prison

Adversity can shake our inner security. It
presses home the question of what motivates us
and can break through the facade of our com-
fortable life. Such questioning need not be
destructive, but it may well reveal how mixed
our inner impulses are. We may appear brave
when in fact we are afraid, bold when we are
really apprehensive, and strong when we feel
ourselves to be weak. Such conflicts, when
openly acknowledged, should make us more
careful about our strengths and more prayerful
about our weaknesses.

Psalm 55: 6-8 and 22   **January 14**

Facing up to difficulty

'There are two ways of dealing with adversity. One way, the easier, is to ignore it altogether. I have got about as far as that. The other and more difficult way is to face up to it and triumph over it. I can't manage that yet, but I must learn to do it.'

Letters and Papers from Prison

Difficulty is always peculiarly our own. Another person looking on will probably fail to appreciate the extent of the pressure that such adversity brings us. But we can't carry the difficulty on our own. Being alone in it will only intensify it. But others can't rescue us, either. We need to face it ourselves, seek God's intervention and support, and open it to others so that they might encourage us to see it through to the end.

MEDITATION: *Difficulty is not outside of God's design for our lives, but God is never outside the difficulty unless we put him there.*

Matthew 6: 6   **January 15**

Prayer

'But when all's said and done, it is true that it needs trouble to drive us to prayer, though every time I feel it is something to be ashamed of.'

Letters and Papers from Prison

Prayer is one of the most difficult but also one of the most rewarding disciplines of the Christian life. It is difficult because we find it easier to do than ask, to act than to be still and to talk than to listen. But prayer is rewarding since it never fails to catch God's ear, lay bare our desires, rightly acknowledge our limitations and subtly transform us into becoming more God-conscious and less self-reliant.

THOUGHT: *Prayer invites God into the very fabric of our lives and into situations of concern.*

Reality and grace

'It is only when one knows the ineffability of the name of God that one can utter the name of Jesus Christ. It is only when one loves life and the earth so much that without them everything would be gone, that one can believe in the resurrection and a new world. It is only when one submits to the law that one can speak of grace, and only when one sees the anger and wrath of God hanging like grim realities over the head of one's enemies that one can know something of what it means to love them and forgive them.'

Letters and Papers from Prison

We can accept God's good gifts too easily. Grace can be accepted only when we face our own inabilities. Forgiveness can be embraced only when we lay bare our wrongdoing, and hope can be imparted only when we face the reality of our own despair.

MEDITATION: *Genuine gifts are for those who acknowledge genuine needs.*

Interruptions and opportunities

'We must be ready to allow ourselves to be interrupted by God. . . It is a strange fact that Christians and even ministers frequently consider their work so important and urgent that they will allow nothing to disturb them. They think they are doing God a service in this, but actually they are disdaining God's "crooked yet straight path". '

Life Together

Our work is never unimportant. In it we express our responsibility for God's world. But our work should never be so important that we fail to be flexible and open to adjustment. It is no less so with spiritual service. In fact, sensitivity to interruptions may provide opportunities to express God's care and intervention in our world.

THOUGHT: *If we are working for the God who never sleeps and who is ever sustaining all of life, we should not be surprised that he requires that we be flexible, sensitive and open to redirection.*

The second Adam

'Jesus Christ is for his brethren by standing in their place.'

Christology

Jesus has taken his stand in the place where I should be standing but have failed. He was obedient where I refused to listen. He was faithful where I was wayward. He was resolute where I wavered. He was forgiving where I was bitter. He pleased his Father where I pleased myself. He bore my sin and shame while I was the guilty party. Yet, surprisingly, he welcomes and embraces me and empowers me to become like him.

MEDITATION: *If Christ would not be for us, who then* would *be?*

Life's goal

'The essence of chastity is not the suppression of lust, but the total orientation of one's life towards a goal.'

Letters and Papers from Prison

In the final analysis, the key issue is not whether we are married or unmarried, a missionary or a motor mechanic. The more important issue is that we have made some sense of God's call in our lives. For that call to be realisable, we need to understand ourselves sufficiently so that we know our gifts, motivations, strengths and weaknesses. When God's call harmonises with our giftedness, we become candidates for lasting achievement.

PRAYER: *Lord, grant that whatever I may need to lay aside to fulfil your will may not be seen as a sacrifice, but rather as the pathway to true achievement. Amen.*

More than reasonable

'One is distressed by the failure of reasonable people to perceive either the depths of evil or the depths of the holy.'

Ethics

In our desire to be good witnesses of Jesus Christ, we assume that we need to be decent citizens. This generally means that we should be tolerant, reasonable and polite. But this must never mean that we compromise and are afraid to stand up for what is just and right. If we are to celebrate the good, we must stand against evil in our lives and in our world. The Christian surely must be a person of passion rather than of reasonableness.

THOUGHT: *Reasonable people maintain the world. Passionate people change it.*

Encountering Jesus

'In the end, there are only two possibilities of en-
countering Jesus: either man must die or he kills
Jesus.'

Christology

To be confronted by Jesus through the words
of the gospel is usually a disturbing experience.
For we see in him what we should be but frequently are not. For what he said and did has
such a ring of truth about it, that it challenges
us to leave our mediocrity and embrace his
vision of excellence. This vision is none other
than the way of servant leadership. In embracing Christ, we must abandon our own way. In
abandoning Christ, we maintain the folly of our
own wisdom.

MEDITATION: *The relinquishment of the old is the
way to embrace the opportunities of the new.*

Each new day

'The first moments of the new day are not the time for our own plans and worries, not even for our zeal to accomplish our own work, but for God's liberating grace, God's sanctifying presence.'

Meditating on the Word

To acknowledge the presence of God at the start of each day before we encounter our family, friends and workmates not only gives God the right priority, but more adequately equips us to serve our fellow man. Our first act is not to do, but to believe; not to give, but to receive; not to speak, but to listen; and not to perform, but to pray.

THOUGHT: *The person who waits to hear from God may in the long run walk more swiftly.*

When there is no resolution

'Nothing can fill the gap when we are away from those we love. . . It is nonsense to say that God fills the gap: he does not fill it, but keeps it empty so that our communion with another may be kept alive, even at the cost of pain.'

Letters and Papers from Prison

God never promises to soothe every pain, resolve every difficulty, heal every heartache and fill every void in our lives. The unresolved issues in our lives become the opportunity for us to pray, persevere, adjust and grow to become more open, caring, patient and giving.

PRAYER: *Lord, in the times of loneliness and difficulty, help me not to press you for easy solutions which provide relief but no growth and no long-term resolution. Amen.*

Lord, speak to me

'In our meditation, we ponder the chosen text on
the strength of the promise that it has something utterly personal to say to us for this day and for our
Christian life that is not only God's word for the
church, but also God's word for us individually.'

Life Together

Scripture is God's word for the church of all
ages and places. But God always addresses us
personally. He calls me to listen and obey. He
challenges me to live in integrity and faithfulness. He calls me to be moral and upright.
What binds us together as Christians is that we
are all seeking individually to respond to
Christ's words for our lives.

MEDITATION: *When God speaks to me personally, I
become responsible for my response.*

Those wandering thoughts

'If your thoughts keep wandering, there is no need for you to hold onto them compulsively. There is nothing wrong with letting them roam where they will, but then incorporate in your prayers the place or person to which they have gone.'

Meditating on the Word

In our prayers and meditations we frequently experience our thoughts running off in various directions. At times we may need to rein in those thoughts to focus on what is important. Yet at other times, those seemingly wayward thoughts can lead us to pray for persons and situations that we normally would not have considered, but which are important in God's scheme of things.

PRAYER: *Holy Spirit, lead me in my praying and reflecting to those persons, issues and concerns that are of your choosing. Amen.*

Strength to live by

'Has the fellowship served to make the individual free, strong and mature, or has it made him weak and dependent? Has it taken him by the hand for a while in order that he may learn again to walk by himself, or has it made him uneasy and unsure?'

Life Together

The Christian individual needs the fellowship of other Christians to be strengthened and encouraged. This fellowship, however, should not breed dependence. Nor should it make us inward-looking. True fellowship should empower us to be bold and take risks for the sake of Jesus Christ and should prepare us to face life in all its challenges.

MEDITATION: *To really serve the other is to encourage that person to live life boldly and freely.*

❧

Christ the centre

'Christ is indeed the centre of human existence, the centre of history and now, too, the centre of nature.'

Christology

We confess that Jesus Christ, the carpenter from Nazareth, is Lord of our lives. He is also the head of the church. But the significance of Jesus cannot be relegated simply to the personal and the ecclesiastical. We must also see Jesus as Lord of all life. He has relevance for the political and economic aspects of life as well. Our challenge is to apply his words to every area of life and to pray that his Spirit may permeate everything we do.

PRAYER: *Lord Jesus, send your Spirit to renew us and all the structures and institutions of our world. Amen.*

Pressing the Bible for answers

'One cannot simply read the Bible the way one reads other books. One must be prepared to really question it. Only then will it open itself up. Only when we await the final answer from the Bible will it be given to us.'

Meditating on the Word

The Bible is God's divine recipe for life. It teaches us God's wisdom. It challenges us to make God's concerns central to our lives. But the Bible does not yield its riches easily. It needs to be mined for its wisdom and pressed for its answers. An attitude which seeks and which longs to know the mind of God is therefore essential to hearing what God might say to us.

THOUGHT: *The more penetrating our questions the more profound the answers will be. The secret of true wisdom is to ask those questions that lead to understanding.*

Life to the full

'We can have a full life even when we haven't got everything we want.'

Letters and Papers from Prison

The quality of our lives does not depend on the abundance of material possessions. Life derives its quality from our hopes, aims, ambitions and strength of character. Some people always worry about whether they have enough and do very little. Others are excited about turning the little they have into much. It is more important to plan to do things with what we have than to spend time worrying about what we haven't got.

MEDITATION: *Those who use even the little things they have will always gain, although it may not always be in kind.*

Challenge to our values

'In a world where success is the measure and justification of all things, the figure of him who was
sentenced and crucified remains a stranger and is at
best the object of pity.'

Ethics

Power and success are the sought-after com-
modities of our age. Jesus poses a radical challenge to our ideas about these concerns. His
idea of success is to faithfully accomplish the
Father's will in his concern for justice, mercy
and peace. And his idea of power is that we exercise it over our own lives in order to serve the
other better, rather than that we exercise power
over others to favour our own ends.

THOUGHT: *Jesus ever poses a threat to our values
and priorities.*

Order in the Christian life

'It is wrong to say that we are being "legalistic" when we are concerned with the ordering of our Christian life and with our faithfulness in requirements of scripture reading and prayer. Disorder undermines and destroys the faith.'

Meditating on the Word

Our spirituality finds its origin in the grace and love of God and the enrichment which the Spirit brings to our lives. What the Spirit does is not devoid of order and our response is not without its structures. The issue is never one of form versus freedom or Spirit versus structure or spontaneity versus routine, but has everything to do with faithfulness and consistency. For this we need the Spirit's help and our own appropriate routines.

MEDITATION: *Spirituality without discipline is like a river without its banks.*

February

The only man who has the right to say that he is justified by grace alone is the man who has left all to follow Jesus.

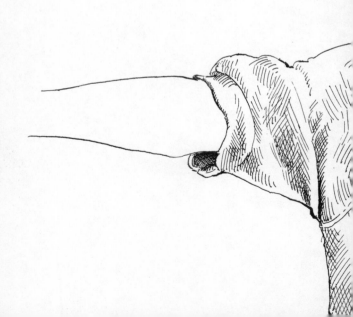

Faith and obedience

'The only man who has the right to say that he is
justified by grace alone is the man who has left all
to follow Jesus.'

The Cost of Discipleship

The life that God gives us in his Son is a life
that came at the cost of death. That life is freely
offered to us and is received by faith in Jesus
Christ. But that life does not leave us where we
are. It is not simply an additive. The life that
Christ brings is transforming. It moves us from
where we are to where we ought to be. It calls
us to leave our own way. It calls us to walk in
the way of Christ.

MEDITATION: *Great gifts come at a costly price and
receiving such gifts is also costly for the recipient.*

Overcoming death

'Two things have become important to me recently: death is outside us, and it is in us. Death from outside is the fearful foe which comes to us when it will. . . But the other death in us — it is our own death. . . We die to it when we love Christ and the brethren.'

The Way to Freedom

Physical death faces each one of us. For some it comes prematurely. For others it comes belatedly at the end of a full life. Such a death comes once only. But a daily death is also with us. This is a death that comes when we forsake God, neglect the way of righteousness and live in disobedience and unforgiveness. The first death is overcome in the resurrection. The second must be daily overcome through the life that Christ gives us through his Spirit.

PRAYER: *Lord, grant that I may always choose life that comes from faith and obedience in the life of Christ.*

The art of receiving

'In normal life we hardly realise how much more we receive than we give, and life cannot be rich without such gratitude.'

Letters and Papers from Prison

We have received life. What we have learned, others have taught us. What we do particularly well is due to the talents and gifts that God has entrusted to us. We are surrounded by family and friends who have enriched our lives in various ways. Much has been given to us. But we receive more when we are thankful for all that God and others have given us.

THOUGHT: *Unthankfulness robs us of the benefits of the very things we have received.*

Unmasking our traditions

'The real trouble is that the pure word of Jesus has been overlaid with so much human ballast — burdensome rules and regulations, false hopes and consolations — that it has become extremely difficult to make a genuine decision for Christ.'

The Cost of Discipleship

The church with its traditions does not always enhance the reality of Christ. It sometimes masks it. It does this particularly when it elevates tradition over scripture, law over grace, and human opinion over the obedient listening to God's voice. The church can never know better than what Christ has revealed to us in the Gospels. It can only seek to hear, obey and live out those words. When the church does this, it finds that Christ is present in his love and power.

THOUGHT: *While we may long for the regularity of our traditions, the power of what Christ says, by way of challenge and empowerment, is alone life-giving.*

Not relying on the past

'I do not do something again today because it
seemed to me to be good yesterday, but because the
will of God points out this way to me today.'

No Rusty Swords

We can quite easily begin to live the Christian
life out of habit. We live by the lessons of the
past and draw life from the experiences of
yesterday. While it is important to gain wisdom from the lessons of the past, the past cannot sustain the present. For the present we
need new grace, inspiration and direction.

THOUGHT: *Your mercies, O Lord, are new every
morning.*

The One who has gone before

'God's ways are the ways which he himself has gone and which we are now to go with him. God will not allow us to go on any way which he himself has not preceded us.'

Meditating on the Word

Jesus is the One who has gone in front of us. He has led the way. He has entered the human arena and experienced all the challenges and difficulties of life that we are likely to experience. He did not always find this easy. In fact, he learned obedience through the things he suffered. Yet he remained the faithful Son of the Father. His perseverance encourages and empowers us as we draw inspiration from his life through the Holy Spirit to live in faithfulness and obedience.

MEDITATION: *Jesus is ahead of us, even beyond the realm of death. He made it. So can we — through him.*

Celebration

'Our life is not only travail and labour; it is also refreshment and joy in the forgiveness of God. We labour, but God nourishes and sustains us. And this is the reason for celebrating.'

Life Together

Our daily work is not to be outside of God's purpose for our life. The milkman and preacher not only share in the pressures of daily toil, but also in the challenge of making their work part of God's providence and care. Both are to do their work for God. And both are to celebrate God's sustaining hand in their lives and enjoy the fruit of their labour.

THOUGHT: *What would happen to us in our witness and celebration of life if we became so overburdened by our daily activities that we lost the happiness offered by him who, seven times over in the Beatitudes, declared: 'Happy are you'?*

The power of the gospel

'I have noticed that the most effective sermons were those in which I spoke enticingly of the gospel, like someone telling children a story of a strange country.'

No Rusty Swords

The words of Jesus as recorded in the Gospels are strangely powerful. They turn our values upside down. The wise are to be childlike. The powerful are to become servants. The weak are strong. Those who have nothing receive the blessings of the kingdom. The outcasts are welcomed into God's family. Those who acknowledge their sins are forgiven. These words not only challenge us, but invite us to live that kind of reality.

THOUGHT: *The strange words of Jesus call us to experience life in a new way.*

Bread for all

'So long as we eat our bread together, we shall have sufficient even with the least. Not until one person desires to keep his own bread for himself does hunger ensue.'

Life Together

The little or much we have is never for ourselves alone. It is to be shared. If we live for ourselves we may have much, but this will only impoverish us. It is the givers who are rich, for in their giving they invite God's blessing and experience a fellowship with those among whom God has chosen to presence himself — the poor.

MEDITATION: *If we want to show the world that we are serious about creating communion among all people, we must begin by searching for ways of promoting a just distribution of the products of the earth.*

God's benediction

'There are Christians who want to be more spiritual than God himself. They like to talk of battle, renunciation, suffering and the cross, and it is almost painful to them that the holy scripture speaks not only of that, but time and again of the good fortune of the devout, the well-being of the just.'

Meditating on the Word

The Christian life is neither one of self-negation, nor one of unlimited blessing. It is rather living in response to God and facing life's challenges and difficulties in hope, faith and perseverance. The Christian is challenged to be thankful for the blessings and to share those with others. But in adversity and difficulty the Christian is challenged not to blame others, but to trust God to be an ever-present help. It is only when we are enriched by God's benediction that we can face hardship and be generous to others.

THOUGHT: *A hardship mentality can make us narrow and defensive. A success and prosperity mentality can make us selfish. An attitude of thankfulness to God, for what he gives us, can make us truly generous.*

Mutual confession

'In the confession of concrete sins the old man dies a painful, shameful death before the eyes of a brother. Because this humiliation is so hard, we continually scheme to evade confession to a brother.'

Life Together

Confession of our sin is to be made to God. But there are times when our confession should be made in the presence of another person. This is particularly appropriate when we need to confess something that has been a persistent problem in our life, or we need to lay bare something that has been such a burden to us that we find it difficult to believe that God can forgive us. In such cases, the other person can reflect to us something of God's willingness to hear and can grant us the absolution in God's name to encourage our faith in God's grace and pardon.

THOUGHT: *There are times when the good news of God's forgiving love needs to be proclaimed to us.*

Transforming our desires

'Clinging too much to our desires easily prevents us from being what we ought to be and can be.'

Letters and Papers from Prison

There is possibly much that we desire that is good. But everything that is good is not necessarily appropriate as far as God's purpose for our lives is concerned. This is not to suggest that God plans for us something that is less than good. It is rather that he calls us not to desire the good, but to do his will. This will mean relinquishing our good for his greater good. It means that we do not live simply by ethical principles, but more out of a desire to please God in the things we do.

MEDITATION: *Relinquishment is the first step along the way of doing the greater good.*

Confrontation

'Where defection from God's word in doctrine or life imperils the family fellowship and with it the whole congregation, the word of admonition and rebuke must be ventured. Nothing can be more cruel than the tenderness that consigns another to his sin. Nothing can be more compassionate than the severe rebuke that calls a brother back from the path of sin.'

Life Together

Soft healers make gangerous sores, goes an old Dutch proverb. And so it is in the life of the church's fellowship where sin and wrongdoing are not firmly confronted. True love and care for the other does not condone wrongdoing, but risks loving confrontation. Such confrontation must always be done in humility and sometimes with tears.

PRAYER: *Lord, help me first of all to confront in my own life all that is not according to your will. Amen.*

Faith and obedience

'Only he who believes is obedient, and only he who
is obedient believes.'

The Cost of Discipleship

God calls us to embrace his words and his
ways. This is the first call to obedience. It also
remains the last call, for the Christian life is
nothing more or less than a continual response
to God's word and Spirit in faith and
obedience. Faith is not simply accepting that
the things God has revealed are true, but it involves the challenge that we order the whole of
our lives accordingly.

MEDITATION: *Christian belief leads to a relationship and intimacy with God and this intimacy expresses itself in deeds of faith and acts of love.*

Under God's watchful eye

'So be mindful in your actions that you are acting under God's eyes.'

No Rusty Swords

God does not watch over us with cold detachment and legalistic precision. His is the oversight that guides and encourages as well as that which gently corrects us. Our motivation for acting in the world should not be fear of God's correction, but the thrill of being part of God's concern for our world.

PRAYER: *Lord, thank you that your watchful eye over me is one of fatherly concern. Teach me to do what is right, simply because that is the way I desire to live and not because I fear your retribution and correction. Amen.*

The way is clear

'Things are much simpler here than we would prefer. It is not that we do not know God's commandments, but that we do not keep them.'

Meditating on the Word

God calls us to forsake our own ideas and to embrace his. He challenges us to put him first and ourselves last. He draws us to live by his words and to suspect our own worldly wisdom. He maps out the way, rather than leaving us to stumble in the dark. He leads the way and calls us to follow, rather than leaving us to set our own goals. Living our lives God's way is the way of true wisdom.

THOUGHT: *It is not that we don't have enough direction. It is rather that we don't have the right motivation.*

Overcoming evil

'What is worse than doing evil is being evil.'

Ethics

We all make mistakes. We also sin against God and others. When this grieves us and propels us to make things right, then it is the good and not evil that dominates our lives. Making things right with an attitude of humility will make the good grow in our lives. And so we can look to God to transform our repentance into an empowerment to do that which is pleasing in his sight.

THOUGHT: *As evil grows through many small acts of wrongdoing, so good develops as we continue to do what is right before God and others.*

True fellowship

'Many people seek fellowship because they are afraid to be alone. Because they cannot stand loneliness, they are driven to seek the company of other people. There are Christians, too, who cannot endure being alone, who have had some experiences with themselves, who hope they will gain some help in association with others.'

Life Together

True fellowship does not result when we join others in flight from our own needs and loneliness. We then join others as demanders and are soon disappointed when all of our needs are not met. Rather, we should join with others in order to share a common journey, sharing common joys and gifts, sharing common difficulties and sharing a common search to make a better world.

PRAYER: *Lord, may my desire for fellowship grow out of a genuine willingness to serve others in the body of Christ and to receive ministry from others with openness and appreciation. Amen.*

Follow me!

'The disciple is dragged out of his relative security into a life of absolute insecurity — that is, in truth, into the absolute security and safety of the fellowship of Jesus.'

The Cost of Discipleship

Jesus' call takes us away from the ordinary and plunges us into the realm of the extraordinary. It takes us away from our certainties and securities and takes us into the realm of uncertainty. At least so it seems, because our worldly values are so pervasive that they define what is ordinary. But it is also possible that living according to the words of Jesus is the most normal way to live, even though our society does not think so. We will only make this surprising discovery when we are simply doing what Jesus asks of us.

MEDITATION: *The apparent difficulty in living out the words of Jesus is dissolved in the act of obedience.*

The voice of the other

'Therefore, a Christian needs another Christian who speaks God's word to him. He needs him again and again when he becomes uncertain and discouraged, for by himself he cannot help himself without belying the truth. He needs his brother as a bearer and proclaimer of the divine word of salvation.'

Life Together

We are often our own worst enemies. We feed our fears. Deny our abilities. Doubt God's grace and forgiveness. Undermine our confidence. Suppress the promptings of the Spirit. We therefore need others to challenge, confront and encourage us. Through another we can hear the voice of God and receive the words of consolation and challenge that we need to hear.

PRAYER: *Lord, help me, that my difficulties will not drive me further inward to doubt and despair, but outward to embrace the words and love of those you send me on my pathway. Amen.*

Working for our good

'You have granted me many blessings; now let me also accept what is hard from your hand. You will make all things work together for good for your children.'

Prayers from Prison

The ordinary circumstances of life are not outside of God's involvement and planning. God wishes to use many of life's normal situations to mould and shape our lives. Both difficulties and blessings can be used to make us more gentle, godly, sensitive and caring. While blessings can make us complacent and difficulties can make us hard, it is our response to the God of the blessings and the hardships that will cause us to grow through both to become more human and Christlike.

THOUGHT: *It is what we do with blessings or difficulties that will determine the kind of persons we are becoming.*

Certainty in acting

'The nature of this will of God can only be clear in
the moment of action.'

No Rusty Swords

Some people wish to be so sure that what they
are doing is what God asks of them that they
always hesitate and finally shrink from doing
anything. The desire to please God is not at
fault here, but the wish to be totally sure is. We
will never be totally sure unless we are also
prepared to take a step of faith and trust God to
make his will clear. Certainty frequently comes
as we look back on the road we have taken and
discover that God has been guiding us all along
the way.

PRAYER: *Lord, help me to trust that you are with
me and guiding me even though I am not totally
sure. Amen.*

Prayer and work

'Praying and working are two different things. Prayer should not be hindered by work, but neither should work be hindered by prayer... Without the burden and labour of the day, prayer is not prayer, and without prayer work is not work.'

Life Together

Work should never become so all-consuming that no time is left for prayer. Prayer should not draw us away from the reality of life so that we no longer fulfil our duties and responsibilities. Prayer should not alienate us from the world. Work should not draw us away from God. Our prayer should result in work and our work should be sustained by prayer.

MEDITATION: *Piety and worldliness belong together. So does prayer and work, faith and action, withdrawal and participation.*

Religion and life

'The pure teaching of the gospel is not a religious concern, but a desire to execute the will of God for a new creation.'

The Way to Freedom

The teaching of the gospel is not a message that draws us from life into a holy enclave. Instead, it draws us out of the bondage of our own selfishness and sin and frees us to face life with boldness and in faith. The vision of life that the gospel holds before us is never a narrow one. It involves seeking to effect change in family, society, the state and the whole of creation. While this vision is too big for us personally, together we can work for these larger goals, providing we never cease to rely wholly on God.

THOUGHT: *The greater the task, the greater our need for God's grace and empowering.*

Shame and glory

'That body, in which Christ lived in the form of a servant, rose on Easter Day as a new body, with heavenly form and radiance. But if we would have a share in that glory and radiance, we must first be conformed to the image of the suffering servant who was obedient to the death of the cross. If we would bear the image of his glory, we must first bear the image of his shame.'

The Cost of Discipleship

It is simply not true to say that, since Christ has done all the suffering, those who belong to him will only experience the benefits and blessing of that suffering and will never need to suffer themselves. Christ has not only done things for us, but he also does things with us and is the pattern by which we need to order our lives. We will therefore need to walk a similar path to him. Suffering and blessing and honour will also characterise our life.

THOUGHT: *There is no glory without the cross and there is no growth without suffering.*

Growing oaks

'Goodness, beauty and truth. . . and all great accomplishments need time, permanence and memory, or else they deteriorate.'

Letters and Papers from Prison

We need to live for more than short-term goals and quick results. The more useful and lasting things in life usually take time, planning and hard work. To develop important family traditions can take a lifetime. To influence the institutions and structures of our society needs no less a time commitment. Our vision as Christians should not be restricted to the here and now. We should work and pray that we might leave a heritage that will enrich future generations.

MEDITATION: *If I sow righteousness and peace in my lifetime, I could produce a harvest that cannot be measured.*

Response to grace

'They know that where there is grace proclaimed
man is called to "What shall I do?", because otherwise grace becomes a judgment.'

The Way to Freedom

Knowledge brings with it responsibility, and
grace always calls us to a response. God's action towards us is never meant to leave us
where we are, but is a challenge to move us forward. Grace is thus never a convenient gift, but
a disturbing intruder. It is not meant to lull us
into the sleep of certitude, but dynamites our
securities so that we embrace the risk of faith
and the challenge of discipleship.

PRAYER: *Lord, grant that I may learn to respond
concretely and practically to your grace and action
in my life. Amen.*

Listening afresh

'I am going through another spell of finding it difficult to read the Bible. I never know quite what to make of it. I don't feel guilty about it, and I know it won't be too long before I return to it again with renewed zest.'

Letters and Papers from Prison

It is not simply a matter of reading scripture. Scripture is also meant to be understood, digested and acted upon. Thus there are times when reading should give way to reflection and when both should issue in practical action. Yet action can never be sustained by a word of the past. It needs the present word to fuel it. Thus a fresh listening to scripture can never be replaced.

THOUGHT: *God's word can not only sustain us in the tasks of life; it can also inspire us to adopt new tasks and priorities.*

March

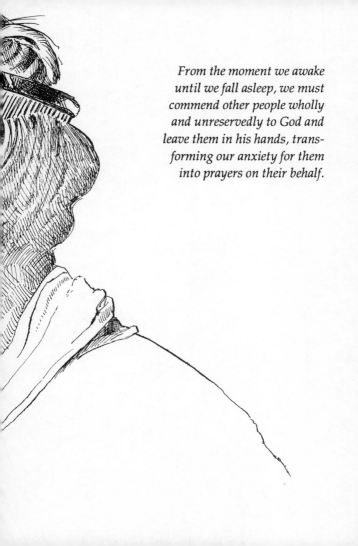

*From the moment we awake
until we fall asleep, we must
commend other people wholly
and unreservedly to God and
leave them in his hands, transforming our anxiety for them
into prayers on their behalf.*

Transforming anxiety into prayer

'From the moment we awake until we fall asleep, we must commend other people wholly and unreservedly to God and leave them in his hands, transforming our anxiety for them into prayers on their behalf.'

Letters and Papers from Prison

There are many times when we are anxious about children, family and friends. There is often much that we worry about — their spiritual well-being, schooling, health, friendships, living arrangements and work. Needless to say, our anxious thoughts are seldom productive and frequently only serve to intensify our level of worry. In seeking to transform anxiety into prayer, it is not simply a matter of talking to God instead of talking to ourselves, for that may simply result in talking anxiously to God. Rather we are challenged to recognise the limitations of our worrying and the possibilities of what trusting prayer can do.

THOUGHT: *Prayer is never simply a matter of talking to God. It is trusting him with our concerns.*

Submission to the authorities

'Resistance and submission are both equally necessary at different times.'

Letters and Papers from Prison

The life and teaching of the biblical prophets and Jesus both show that we are not to accept evil in our world. Evil and injustice need to be shown for what they are and should be resisted and overcome. To condone what is wrong is never a virtue and, if wrong is done by those in authority, this does not make it right. Authorities are to be obeyed when they 'are God's servants to do good'. When they no longer function in this way, they are to be called to account and resisted by every legitimate means.

MEDITATION: *Obedience is never blind, but is a moral response with a view to the implications of our obedience.*

Practical responsibility

'Let no-one say, "God has blessed me with money and possessions," and then live as if he and his God were alone in the world.'

No Rusty Swords

What we have has been given even if we have earned it, because our abilities and skills, even life itself, are gifts. This is true for all us. Therefore what we have has come as part of our solidarity with others. If we don't receive anything apart from our involvement with others, then we certainly ought to give something in return as an expression of that involvement. This giving should not be preferential; it is not simply for friends of the Christian community. Our giving should be for all, for all are made in God's image and the cry of the needy knows no boundaries of creed or race. There is nothing particularly special about giving; it is simply a recognition of our responsibility to others.

PRAYER: *Lord, help me to see that what I have has been received and this makes a claim on me to be generous and not to hold things simply to myself. Amen.*

The priority of prayer

'Wasted time which we are ashamed of, temptations that beset us, weakness and listlessness in our work, disorder and indiscipline in our thinking and our relations with other people very frequently have their cause in neglect of the morning prayer. The organisation and distribution of our time will be better for having been rooted in prayer.'

Life Together

Prayer is the time to be still. It is a way to reflect. It is a time to be honest. It is the time for confession. It is the way by which we may seek God's help, wisdom and strength. It is the way to listen. It is the avenue for fresh inspiration. Little wonder that when we consistently live without this discipline in the Christian life, we lose direction, power and purpose.

THOUGHT: *For the busy person, prayer is never an option that can be dispensed with, but the source of power and perseverance.*

Participating in life

'I ought to behave myself like a guest here, with all that entails. I should not stay aloof and refuse to participate in the tasks, joys and sorrows of earth, while I am waiting patiently for the redemption of the divine promise.'

Meditating on the Word

The Christian is not someone who is marking time while waiting for heaven. Our purpose for being does not simply lie in the future life, but particularly in being here. We have a responsibility to participate in all of life. Our participation, however, should not be characterised by an attitude of exploitation, but one of gentle participation that looks beyond the expediency of the present and concerns itself with long-term goals and benefits.

MEDITATION: *Preparation for heaven is not withdrawal and passivity, but a strenuous participation in the challenges of life.*

Perseverance

'A man can hold his own. . . only if he can combine simplicity with wisdom.'

Ethics

Life is not simply about starting new projects and having bursts of energy at the beginning of the things we start. It is also a matter of seeing things through to the end, even in the face of difficulty. To have the wherewithal for the long journey requires that we possess more than brute force. Instead, we need the wisdom of practical experience that will provide us with the understanding to anticipate what may lie ahead. To gain this wisdom, we must plunge into the risk-taking of life and carefully and reflectively learn its lessons.

THOUGHT: *The way of wisdom is the royal road of perseverance.*

The Spirit: gift to the community

'It will again be found in the fact that it pleased the Holy Spirit to promise himself not to the individual, but to the gathering. It is the visible gathering which receives the Spirit and which is brought to *koinonia* through the Spirit.'

The Way to Freedom

No-one has the front edge on the Holy Spirit. Unlike the Old Testament where the Spirit came upon the select few, in this age the Spirit is for all — for women to empower them in ministry, for the young to have their visions, for the old to dream their dreams and for all to experience the Spirit's gifts and fruits. While the Spirit does not empower us all in the same way, we should be wary of those who claim special revelations of the Spirit. It is far more likely that the Spirit will reveal his concerns to the many rather than to the few.

MEDITATION: *The Spirit is Christ's gift to the many and this makes the many, one.*

No regrets

'I look back on the past without any self-reproach and accept the present in the same spirit.'

Letters and Papers from Prison

One of the secrets of being able to face the future with hope is that we do not linger around the 'might-have-beens' of the past. If our past has been positive, we should be thankful. If it has been negative, we are called to be forgiving. But finally the past has to be laid to rest so that we can put our energies into the present which will shape our future.

THOUGHT: *To have no regrets is to have made good choices and to have exercised the ministry of forgiveness.*

In the face of the other

'From God he hears the word: "If you want my goodness to stay with you, then serve your neighbour, for in him God comes to you himself".'

No Rusty Swords

Freely, God's goodness comes to us. But God's good gifts do place us under obligation. This obligation has nothing to do with trying to pay God back. That is simply impossible. But God's good gifts affect us and transform us in such a way that we desire to become like the Giver. In expressing this desire, we aim to treat others in the same way that God has treated us.

MEDITATION: *In serving the least of our brothers, we find the gentle approval of the Man of Sorrows.*

Being your own person

'Alone you stood before God when he called you; alone you had to answer that call; alone you had to struggle and pray; and alone you will die and give an account to God.'

Life Together

The Christian community is not the place where we can lose ourselves. We need to be our own men and women before God. As such we join the life of the church, not to run away from anything and least of all to run away from ourselves. Instead, having found who we are in the light of God's redeeming love in Christ Jesus, we join the community to be enriched by it and to serve others in it. This fellowship will aid us in our journey, but should never take away our responsibility to face the challenges of life and the loneliness of death.

PRAYER: *Lord, grant that I may ever have the courage to face you and the challenge of life. Help me not to hide or rationalise and not to seek personal security above the doing of your will. Amen.*

The will of God

'Of course, not everything that happens is the will of God, yet in the last resort nothing happens without his will.'

Letters and Papers from Prison

We cannot trace everything that happens directly back to God's will. Things also happen as a result of our own willing and doing. Things also occur as a result of the pervasive evil of our world. God is not causally responsible for everything, for that would eliminate human freedom and responsibility. But he is concerned about everything that happens. He is also providentially involved in all that takes place. And we are assured that all things do finally work for good for those who love God.

THOUGHT: *In hindsight, we can often see that God was much more closely involved in our actions than we had first thought.*

Being thankful for the small things

'Only he who gives thanks for little things receives the big things. We prevent God from giving us the great spiritual gift he has in store for us, because we do not give thanks for daily gifts. We think we dare not be satisfied with the small measure of spiritual knowledge, experience and love that has been given to us.'

Life Together

Being thankful for the small things does not mean that we simply settle for small things. We can dream and work towards the greater and more significant. But these things don't come our way by grasping after them. The greater comes from the process of growth and growth always has its small beginnings. It is our positive and thankful response to the seemingly small things that sets us on the road to greater achievement.

PRAYER: *Lord, grant that in the small things I may be thankful and in the big things I may not lose my appreciation of what you do. Amen.*

Fruitful engagement

'Today I am able to take a calmer view of other people, of their needs and requirements, and so I am able to help them more.'

Letters and Papers from Prison

We can become overwhelmed by the needs of others. Needs can be so pressing that we are driven to frenetic responses. We throw ourselves into the role of helper, but fail to evaluate whether our helping is effective. It is therefore important that we take time to be still, to stand back, to evaluate, to pray and to strategise so that our activity can be better focussed. To lose ourselves in the busyness of much doing is simply to deny our own need to be replenished. To be more discerning, to prioritise and to realise the limits of what we can do will, in fact, help us to be more effective.

THOUGHT: *Busyness does not guarantee productivity and effectiveness.*

For everyone

'God goes to every man with sore bestead, feeds body and spirit with his bread; for Christians, pagans alike he hangs dead, and both alike forgiving.'

Prayer from Prison

God's grace and forgiveness know no cultural, social, ethnic and political boundaries. God's love is for everyone. Sadly, we don't always live by this dictum. We often live our lives in such a way that we reflect the opposite message: 'God's love is only for the few, for those who are like us.' And our practical demonstration of that is our failure to link up with the poor and the disadvantaged in our society. If God comes to every person with his bread, then surely he requires that we be the waiters and the waitresses.

PRAYER: *Father, grant that our lives will become so transformed from our narrow concerns that we will embrace your generous attitude to the world. Amen.*

In the world, but not of the world

'Christians live like other men: they get married, they mourn and rejoice, they buy their requirements and use the world for the purpose of day-to-day existence. But they have everything through Christ alone, in him and for his sake.'

The Cost of Discipleship

In many ways, Christians are no different from others in the way they live. Yet in another way they are very different. This difference is reflected not only in the acknowledgment of Jesus Christ as Lord, but also in the attempt to make the life of Jesus normative for their lives. This results in the Christian being out-of-step with this world's agenda and in step with the mandate of Christ whose concern was to see God's rulership and grace established in the world.

THOUGHT: *The essence of being different does not lie in externals, but in a different internal reality that cannot but manifest itself.*

The concrete word

'Christ. . . is truth spoken in the concrete moment, the address which puts a man in the truth before God.'

Christology

Jesus does not confront us with possibilities and probabilities. Nor is his word to us a list of general principles. Jesus does not even present us with a theological system. Instead, his is the word that disturbs, challenges and calls us to a new way of being and acting. The word that Jesus speaks is never an abstract word; it is one that he himself has lived out. His spoken word is made concrete in his own person. As the living word, then, he confronts us in the spoken and written word to make that word concrete in our own life and actions.

THOUGHT: *There is nothing more powerful than a word that is fleshed out in action.*

Lovers of the dream

'He who loves his dream of a community more than the Christian community itself becomes a destroyer of the latter, even though his personal intentions may be ever so honest and earnest and sacrificial.'

Life Together

There is nothing wrong with having ideals. In fact we can hope for much. But hopes and ideals are not always realised. In holding to our ideals, we need to be careful that we don't hold them in such a way that they take priority over people and that our 'vision splendid' draws us away from facing life realistically. Moreover, our ideals should never be realised at any cost. They are not worth having if they destroy others in the process of their actualisation.

PRAYER: *Lord, grant that I may love people in specific ways and not simply humanity in general. Amen.*

When everything has been done

'I think we ought to do all in our power to alter these facts while there is still time and then, when all our efforts have proved fruitless, it becomes easier to endure them.'

Letters and Papers from Prison

We want to see changes take place in our world, particularly changes to situations which perpetuate evil and injustice. Sadly, we are often slow to act because we avoid seeing things for what they really are. Thus we wait until evil becomes more magnified before we will respond. And then we may claim that it is too late to do anything. But it is never too late to act. Better to act and not be successful than never to have responded at all.

MEDITATION: *Faithfulness can never be measured in terms of success, but only in terms of commitment.*

Unintended consequences

'In carrying through the prohibition law in the 18th Amendment. . . American Christianity. . . has had to recognise that the transference of Christian principles to state life has led to a catastrophic breakdown. The prohibition law gave an unprecedented impulse to crime in the larger cities.'

No Rusty Swords

Sometimes Christians assume that if only they were in power the world would be a better place. But the personal values that Christians hold aren't so easily translated into social values and laws. And more particularly, good social initiatives can have unintended consequences. The complexity of all of this, however, should not reduce us to social inactivism. Christians also have a responsibility to work for a better world. What should characterise us is a willingness to experiment, do our homework, work for gradual change, recognise that there aren't easy answers and display a humility marked by wisdom.

THOUGHT: *Is it better for us to be salt than to have power?*

Grace and transformation

'The justification of the sinner in the world degenerated into the justification of sin and the world. Costly grace was turned into cheap grace without discipleship.'

The Cost of Discipleship

The grace of God never leaves us where we are, but transforms us into living a new set of values. We are justified and forgiven in Christ so that we will live for him and leave behind the idols of our previous lifestyle. Receiving the grace of God never means that we continue with the way things were before. It separates us from the old; it never justifies the old. It embraces the new and calls the old into question. It celebrates the new life in Christ and rejects the value of our previous priorities.

PRAYER: *Lord, may your grace and your action toward me solidify in me a new set of values which expresses itself in new choices and actions. Amen.*

The question of relevance

'The thing that keeps coming back to me is: What *is*
Christianity, and indeed what is Christ, for us
today?'

Letters and Papers from Prison

Christianity never exists in its pure form. It always expresses itself in particular cultural
forms. Because cultures and societies change, a
particular form of Christianity may become irrelevant. The question then becomes a pressing
one: What is Christianity for us today? The
question of relevance is thus ever before us.
The particular form of Christianity that the
Pilgrim Fathers had when they settled the
Americas or the Christian concerns of the
Puritans are no longer our concerns. We live in
a different age and need to struggle with the
question: What does Jesus mean for us today?
How can his death, resurrection, words and
deeds shape and inform us today as we seek to
live a life of discipleship?

While answers are never easy, even the asking of the question is a step in the right direction.

MEDITATION: *Jesus is not simply the man from Galilee, but also the Lord of history: his life thus has power and relevance for the issues of our modern age.*

True life

'Grace. . . is costly because it costs a man his life,
and it is grace because it gives a man the only true
life.'

The Cost of Discipleship

True life consists of life that has God at its
centre. It is a life that seeks to embrace God's
concerns for our society and the world. It
therefore does not live for itself, but is other-
person regarding and concerned about the
wider issues of our world. This kind of life we
do not possess of ourselves. It is life that is
given through the grace of God in Jesus Christ.
The serving life derives from a life that is
graced by the love of God — and this is true
life.

THOUGHT: *If true life is a gift of God's grace, then
such a life is capable of great thankfulness and great
service.*

The law of limitation

'We come to a clearer and more sober estimate of our own limitations and responsibilities, and that makes it possible for us genuinely to love our neighbours.'

Letters and Papers from Prison

The Christian cannot be and do everything. We are limited. We have certain gifts and qualities and respond to particular issues and concerns. To think that we can do anything and everything is not faith but presumption. In acquiring a better understanding of our gifted-ness and orientation, we can the more fully commit ourselves to serving others in love in ways that express who we are.

MEDITATION: *We can only give what we are, not what we would like to be.*

Prayer: a daily service

'Prayer is not a free-will offering to God. . . we are not free to engage in it according to our own wishes. Prayer is the first divine service in the day.'

Meditating on the Word

Prayer can never be peripheral to our lives. It is an essential part of our relationship with God. If we only pray when we desire to do so, then our prayers will probably be self-centred. If, on the other hand, prayer flows out of our love and commitment to God, then it is far more likely to embrace God's concerns and the concerns of others.

THOUGHT: *Prayer can be the heartbeat of our relationship with God and the dynamism of our concern for others.*

Words of absolution, words of hope

'As the open confession of my sins to a brother in-sures me against self-deception, so, too, the assurance of forgiveness becomes fully certain to me only when it is spoken by a brother in the name of God. Mutual, brotherly confession is given to us by God in order that we may be sure of divine forgiveness.'

Life Together

It is always easier to preach God's message to others than to speak it to ourselves. It is often easier to pray healing prayers for others than to pray for our own well-being. It is also easier to accept God's forgiveness and generosity for others than for ourselves. Thus we need to be preached to, prayed for and encouraged. In the words of forgiveness proclaimed to us by a brother or sister, we hear the voice of our Heavenly Father.

PRAYER: *Thank you, Jesus, that in the words of our brother we can hear you saying, 'Your sins are for-given. Go in peace and sin no more.' Amen.*

Knowing Christ

'I have access to the work of Christ only if I know the person who does this work.'

Christology

What Christ offers us — his salvation, grace, new life and Holy Spirit — does not come apart from a relationship with him. Christ's sacrament and forgiveness cannot be dispensed without a commitment to him. The person and work of Christ cannot be separated. In fact, it is only when we in faith embrace Jesus that we experience his benediction and grace. The greater gift is always the Giver and not what he dispenses.

MEDITATION: *The greatest giving is the giving of oneself, not simply one's possessions.*

Uneasy thankfulness

'We must be prepared for the fact that this winter
seven million people in Germany will find no work,
which means hunger for fifteen to twenty million
people. . . When we sit down this evening to a full
table and say grace and thank God for his goodness. . . we will think that we have not in any way
deserved these gifts more than our hungry brothers
in our town.'

No Rusty Swords

Being thankful for the little or much that we
have is an important part of living life with
meaning and appreciation. But our thankfulness can seldom be pure joy, for it is frequently
tarnished by a knowledge of the lack that
others have and by the struggles of our sense of
responsibility as we seek to respond to the
needs of others.

PRAYER: *Lord, as I seek to live a life of thankfulness,
help me at the same time to express that thankfulness in generosity. Amen.*

Life in the church

'So there is no area of the church which is not wholly and exclusively subject to Christ. It is a dreadful reduction of the New Testament concept if today the church is often seen to have its existence only in preaching and the administration of the sacrament.'
The Way to Freedom

Church is not always an attractive place. It often consists in the repetition of certain ceremonies, worship and sermons. The church can be a far more attractive place than that. But its attractiveness need not lie in making those ceremonies more tantalising. It should lie in expanding the notion of what it means to be church. Church is the life together of those who belong to Christ and who meet together — not only for common worship, but also for companionship, hospitality, friendship, common concerns and participating in the joys and struggles of life.

MEDITATION: *The church is to be a life together. This can never be restricted to the sanctuary, but includes the home, the work-place and the whole of life.*

Struggles in the night

'I should tell how my grim experiences often follow me into the night, and the only way I can shake them off is by reciting one hymn after another and that when I wake up it is generally with a sigh, rather than with a hymn of praise.'

Letters and Papers from Prison

The difficult circumstances of the day can become the nightmares of the night. These circumstances are the more difficult when they are beyond our own willing and choosing. And while our circumstances may not be subject to immediate change, our attitude towards them can be. The struggle thus becomes the battle for the mind. It is here that prayer, hymn singing, meditation and scripture reading may be of help. But these can only be of help if they are not used routinely or magically, but are aids to bring us to a greater peace in God's presence.

THOUGHT: *If we cannot change difficult circumstances, we may be able to change our attitudes and feelings towards these circumstances.*

Centre point

'Daily, quiet reflection on the word of God as it applies to me. . . becomes for one a point of crystallisation for everything which gives interior and exterior order to my life.'

Meditating on the Word

Scripture can be more than the rule of faith. It can also be the source of meaning which inspires all our willing, planning, acting and serving in the world. Scripture's history, personalities, stories, prophets, precepts, wisdom and challenges can all become a source of inspiration to me as I seek to apply them to my life's circumstances.

MEDITATION: *Scripture is the wisdom of God by which I can order my daily life.*

Church

'The church is not a community of souls, as people want to make it today, nor is it simply the proclamation of the gospel. In other words, the church is not just the pulpit, but the real body of Christ on earth.'

The Way to Freedom

The church is not simply a spiritual reality. It is a physical institution as well. But it is also more. It is the life of Christ expressed in our world. But this is only the case when we are linked to Christ in faith and obedience, are enlivened by his Spirit, and live out his call to discipleship and mission. For the church to be the body of Christ, it must continue the work and mission of him who called it into being.

MEDITATION: *Christ is present in the world where people proclaim his name and live out his call.*

April

The. . . service that one should perform for another in a Christian community is that of active helpfulness. This means, initially, simple assistance in trifling, external matters.

The same service that one should prefer to her mother in
a Christian community is that of active helpfulness.
This means initially simple assistance in
trifling, external matters.

The simplicity of service

'The. . . service that one should perform for another
in a Christian community is that of active helpfulness. This means, initially, simple assistance in trifling, external matters.'

Life Together

The Christian community is there where Christians meet for fellowship, where they work
together and live in families or as households of
singles. Each particular situation yields its opportunity for acts of kindness and service that
enhance the well-being of the other person.
Acts of service should never be thought of
simply as being the traditional forms of ministry, such as preaching, teaching, healing or
counselling. Acts of service involve the whole
gamut of care, encouragement and helpfulness.
Since acts of service know no limit, everyone
can work in ways that build up others.

MEDITATION: *Service is the crown of the Christian
life.*

In Christ

'Just as Christ is present as the word in the word, as the sacrament in the sacrament, so too he is also present as community and in the community.'

Christology

For the Christian, everything is to find its meaning in Christ. And everything apart from him, no matter how good, holy, religious and significant it may appear to be, is ultimately of little value, for it will lead us to idolatry or to despair. In the Bible, it is Christ that we are to seek. In the sacrament, it is Christ that we encounter by faith. And in the life of the Christian community, it is Christ by his Spirit who must enliven us lest we live on the depletable resources of human relationships and religious forms and ceremonies.

PRAYER: *Lord, apart from you I am nothing and have nothing that will be of lasting significance. Cause me to live out of the fullness of your grace and empowerment. Amen.*

Freedom

'The man who surrenders freedom surrenders his very nature as a Christian.'

No Rusty Swords

Christ offers us freedom from the power of sin. This freedom motivates us to live in conformity with God's will and purpose. But his gift of freedom never allows us to do our own thing. We might think that freedom has to do with being able to do what we want, but this is actually being trapped in our own wanting and willing. Christ's gift of freedom takes us beyond the limits of our own selfishness and into the realm of God's greater good.

THOUGHT: *To be free to do what Christ asks of us is to do the greater good.*

No escape from the world

'There is no place to which the Christian can withdraw from the world, whether it be outwardly or in the sphere of the inner life. Any attempt to escape from the world must sooner or later be paid for with a sinful surrender to the world.'

Ethics

To withdraw from the world in order to remain pure and holy is a distortion of the meaning of holiness. For holiness has to do with turning towards God in the midst of the world, not separation from the world in order to find God. Moreover, withdrawal from the world always results in the startling discovery that the world is still very much with us, albeit in a different form. Escape is never a solution. Only the grace and power of God keeping us in the midst of life provides the way for us to live.

MEDITATION: *The safest place is not so much where we are but who is keeping us.*

Fullness of life
and discipleship

'I am sure we honour God more if we gratefully accept the life he gives us with all its blessing, loving it and drinking it to the full, grieving deeply and sincerely when we have belittled or thrown away any of the precious things of life.'

Letters and Papers from Prison

Discipleship does not mean that we live a life of deprivation, but rather a life of appreciation, thankfulness and sharing. It is only the person who has drunk deeply at the well of life who can voluntarily lay aside things for the sake of others. But even then, one needs to return again and again to be filled, stimulated and encouraged. Discipleship is not throwing blessings away in order to be able to identify with the poor and needy. It is drawing others in to share in the blessings that God gives.

MEDITATION: *Discipleship has nothing to do with throwing things away, but has everything to do with using our gifts and resources with and for others.*

The paradox

> '"Do not hide your commandments from me" is a cry which comes only from the heart of one who knows God's commandments.'
>
> *Meditating on the Word*

Christians live with a constant paradox. They have come 'home', but they are on a journey. They are freed from sin's power, yet daily confess their sins. They have received eternal life, yet wait for the age to come. They know God in the face of Jesus Christ, yet seek him. This tension of the 'now' and 'not yet' is characteristic of the Christian, for having tasted something of the power of the age to come, the Christian awaits the fullness of a kingdom which is still to be revealed.

PRAYER: *Father, grant that in joyfully accepting what I have, I may yet restlessly press for the more that may yet be given. Amen.*

A different love

'Because spiritual love does not desire but rather serves, it loves an enemy as a brother. It originates neither in the brother, nor in the enemy, but in Christ and his word. Human love can never understand spiritual love, for spiritual love is from above; it is something completely strange, new and incomprehensible to all earthly love.'

Life Together

We tend to love those who love us. A love that serves the enemy and thus expects nothing in return for itself is a quality of love that does not come naturally. This kind of love can only be given to us. Christ through the empowerment of his Spirit desires to weave such a capacity in the fabric of our lives. But we will never know the extent of this capacity until we risk to use it.

THOUGHT: *The nature of love is much more a doing than a feeling.*

Real love

'Christ did not, like a moralist, love a theory of good, but he loved the real man.'

Ethics

Like others, the Christian also builds up systems of ethics and principles for being and acting in the world. There is nothing wrong with developing such systems. The only problem is that we can become more concerned with maintaining our systems than in genuinely caring for those whom our systems are meant to serve. It is always easier to be committed to principles than to be involved with the needs of real people.

THOUGHT: *It is more appropriate to get our hands dirty in the service of others than for us to have all our principles intact, but our hearts closed to the act of love and care.*

In the image of God

'Man only knows who he is in the light of God.'

Christology

If God has made us in his own image and if he has made us to live in fellowship with him and to the praise of his glory, then we cannot truly know ourselves or life's purpose without living in the light of God's word and presence. To live in the light of God's ways is thus not a deflection from being truly human. Instead, it is fully realising our 'humanness' with its spiritual dimension. God's presence is not meant to dominate us, but to guide us. God's presence is not meant to blind us, but to enlighten us, so that we can see truly and so live more truly.

PRAYER: *Lord, grant that in my search for meaning and purpose I may constantly seek your wisdom. Amen.*

Principles and flexibility

'There is simply no possibility of erecting generally valid principles, because each moment, lived in God's sight, can bring an unexpected decision.'

No Rusty Swords

There are general moral principles. Murder, for example, is always forbidden for the Christian. Yet the Christian does not simply live by the moral law. Christians also live by the grace of God and by the influence of the Holy Spirit. Thus, while bounded by the moral law, the Christian's response can always be creative, spontaneous and impregnated by a grace that makes our acting a higher righteousness than simply the literal fulfilment of the law.

MEDITATION: *Grace is not in conflict with law, but always supersedes it.*

Our face to the future

'Once a man has found God in his earthly bliss and
thanked him for it, there will be plenty of opportunities for him to remind himself that these earthly
pleasures are only transitory, and that it is good for
him to accustom himself to the idea of eternity.'

Letters and Papers from Prison

Life here ought to be embraced, celebrated and
thankfully appreciated. We are not to reject
fully entering life in this world so that we can
appreciate heaven more. In the full pursuit of
life with all its blessings, challenges and
responsibilities, however, we need to realise
that life is more than what we presently make
of it. It also has a future. It looks for the fulfilment of God's new heaven and earth. That future hope should affect the way we do things
and the choices we make in the present.

THOUGHT: *The hope for heaven should not take us
away from the concerns of the earth, but ought to
make our concerns deeper and more urgent.*

A 'worldly' Christianity

'In Christ he finds God and the world reconciled. . .
His worldliness does not divide him from Christ,
and his Christianity does not divide him from the
world.'

Ethics

The Christian constantly lives in a series of tensions between one reality and another. There is the tension between the reality of the things that are and the things of faith. There is also the tension between being worldly-wise and spiritually true; between being relevant and faithful; and between longing for heaven, yet working actively for change on earth. These tensions will probably be permanently with us. But Christ's incarnation does point the way for us. There God embraced both the world and sought to redeem it.

THOUGHT: *If the world is the object of God's redeeming concern, then we can hardly live as though the world is irrelevant.*

Serving God and our brothers and sisters

'In Jesus, the service of God and the service of the least of the brethren were one.'

The Cost of Discipleship

We like to keep our categories distinct and separate, and therefore manageable. Serving God is not the same as serving the church. And serving the church is not the same as serving the world. Moreover, ministering to our neighbour is not the same as serving our brothers and sisters in the Christian community. Having made these distinctions, the assumption is that we will apportion equal time and energy to each area. In reality, we do not. Moreover, our distinctions are artificial. Our brother is also our neighbour and our neighbour is also our potential brother. More specifically, we are hardly serving God if we are not serving our fellow human beings.

THOUGHT: *In the least of our brothers and sisters we often find the wisdom and grace of God.*

Suffering in the world

'This love of God does not withdraw from reality into noble souls secluded from the world. It experiences and suffers the reality of the world in all its hardness.'

Ethics

Jesus fully entered the world with its political intrigue, religious hypocrisy and social injustice. His was never the longing for a secluded religious community. He healed, dined with sinners, proclaimed his message, made friends, caused trouble with the religious leaders, prayed, travelled and gave hope to the poor. But this simple yet authentic response was too threatening. The world could not tolerate such an existence. It asks for either compromise or death. And since compromise could not be given, death had to be embraced in order to show the worldliness of the world in all its starkest colours. We also cannot simply love in this world. We also will be forced to compromise or to experience rejection.

MEDITATION: *The true nature of the world is seen in its response to true love.*

Nothing is lost

'What does "bring again" mean? It means that nothing is lost, everything is taken up again in Christ. . . Christ brings it all again as God intended it to be, without the distortion which results from human sin.'

Letters and Papers from Prison

The miracle of God's grace extended to us in Jesus is that nothing is ever lost. The life we led before we came to Christ is not lost, but is cleansed and re-incorporated into God's purposes. Our mistakes and wrong decisions while living the Christian life are not lost either. They can be forgiven and can become part of God's way to instruct us and to shape our lives.

PRAYER: *Father, help me not to keep any aspect of my life away from your redeeming grace. Amen.*

Contributing to the well-being of the church

'Every member serves the whole body, either to its health or to its destruction.'

Life Together

The church is a living organism, a body. Its main identity is not found in its formal structures, but in its relationship with Christ and with each other. In building relationships of freedom, encouragement and care as the basis from which to serve each other, we contribute to the health of the whole body. In our failure or unwillingness to do this, we are forced to rely on the church's formal structures which, in themselves, cannot produce the life that Christ wishes to give us. In re-discovering the personal dimension of what it means to be church, we can find creative ways to encourage and build up each other.

THOUGHT: *In the church I can be a taker or a contributor, a blessing or a burden, a participant or an observer.*

Self and others

'When we want to calculate just how much we have
learnt ourselves and how much we owe to others, it
is not only un-Christian, but useless.'

Letters and Papers from Prison

Our life cannot totally depend on others. This
would breed dependence and undermine our
own sense of dignity and responsibility. Instead, we need to find a balance between being
our own persons with a strong sense of self-
identity and purpose and being open to the
contribution, input and encouragement of
others. While we need to be responsible for the
choices and decisions we make, we should always be open to and thankful for the contribution of others.

PRAYER: *Lord, thank you for the way you have
made me and the gifts you have given to me. Help
me to use them, but help me also to be open to grow
through the encouragement of others. Amen.*

Surrendered to God

'Christian ethical action is action for freedom, action from the freedom of a man who has nothing of himself and everything of his God.'

No Rusty Swords

The person who is truly free is the person who is surrendered to God. The person who has placed his hopes, aspirations, plans, abilities, future and resources into the hands of God is the person who is truly free. This freedom from our own concerns and burdens — for our very life has been committed to God — frees us for actions on behalf of others. Sometimes that action may be prayer. At other times it may be costly service.

THOUGHT: *The person who is free from self-concern is free for others.*

Waiting for the kingdom

'So between the death of Christ and the Last Day it is only by the gracious anticipation of the last things that Christians are privileged to live in visible fellowship with other Christians.'

Life Together

In the joining together with other Christians to pray, hear the scriptures, worship, serve and fellowship, we keep alive in our hearts the flame of hope of the age to come where Christ will be all in all. It is in banding together that our life is nurtured, our hope sustained and our faith encouraged. In being together, we share the promise that Christ is in our midst and his Spirit indwells our hearts and our community. In sharing life together, we anticipate the banquet of God's fully established kingdom.

MEDITATION: *The body of Christ consisting of very ordinary people is very special because of its hope in the things yet to come.*

Head and heart

'Teaching about Christ begins in silence.'
Christology

Knowing Christ has everything to do with acknowledging him with our mind. To know Christ is never an anti-intellectual affair. But knowing Christ is also a matter of the heart. By faith we know him, but by his Spirit we also experience his love and presence. Thus our understanding of Christ also comes from that mysterious work of his Spirit which at times is beyond words. If we think that we contain the living Christ within our words and our theology, we have grasped far less than we realise.

PRAYER: *Lord, may I learn more of you through the eyes and the ears of the heart. Amen.*

Christ the bridge-builder

'There are, therefore, not two spheres, but only the one sphere of the realisation of Christ, in which the reality of God and the reality of the world are united.'

Ethics

In Jesus that which was divided potentially becomes one. Jesus unites Jew and Gentile, poor and rich, male and female. He brings together the present and the future. In him, heaven and earth will be united. He draws the church out of those in the world and sends them back into the world for works of service. He makes our worldliness spiritual and our spirituality relevant to the world. Jesus thus builds bridges where previously there was a chasm.

MEDITATION: *To bring together into a colourful unity that which was previously separated and divided is nothing but a miracle.*

Invitation to the 'good'

'It is very presumptuous and wrongheaded to think that the human being has to become deeply entangled in the guilt of life in order to know life itself, and finally God.'

Meditating on the Word

God's salvation and grace are not extended only to the needy and deviant in our society. The 'good' person also needs the grace of God. While the deviant person needs restoration, the 'good' person needs to find hope and meaning and deliverance from the very goodness that, while it brings favour from our fellow man, is a stumbling-block to the love of God. The issue, finally, is not whether we are 'good' or 'bad' persons in the eyes of society, but whether we are truly experiencing the providential care and saving grace of God.

THOUGHT: *God's line of demarcation runs differently from ours. Those we would include as insiders may well be outsiders in God's scheme of things.*

All things done well

'Those very days which were hard to us, which troubled us and worried us — days which have left behind in us a trace of bitterness — should not fade from our minds today until we have been able to confess humbly and thankfully even of them, "He has done all things well".'

The Way to Freedom

We all experience difficulty. Some is of our own making. Other difficulty is inflicted upon us by others. Difficulty can throw us. It can lead to self-recrimination. It can cause us to blame others. It can even cause us to question God's love and ways. Yet if we are ever going to come to terms with difficulty, we will need to recognise that it is a part of life and that we can learn God's wisdom through such experiences.

THOUGHT: *God's 'all things done well' includes suffering and difficulty.*

So close

'Since fallen man cannot rediscover and assimilate the form of God, the only way is for God to take the form of man and come to him.'

The Cost of Discipleship

The good news of Christianity is not that we find God, but that God finds us. He is already there before we start to seek him. In Christ, God has fully entered our world with all its wonderful possibilities, but also with its shame and degradation. He could not possibly come any closer to us, for he has also entered our struggles and our suffering. He has even taken upon himself the sins that are ours in order to free us. Through this amazing friendship he grants us the possibility of a new life.

PRAYER: *Lord Jesus, thank you for coming to me with your grace and love and for offering your Spirit as the gift of friendship. Amen.*

Strength for the future

'. . .the things we have consciously or unconsciously assimilated will never be forgotten. Intense experience forges them into certainties, convictions and plans for the future so that they become important for our future lives.'

Letters and Papers from Prison

There is much that simply becomes a part of our lives through our upbringing and environment. But it is our conscious and deliberate commitments and choices that give life its particular quality and direction. When those commitments have been tested in the furnace of life's intractability and have endured, then they become an important part of the way we approach the future.

THOUGHT: *Tested and proved convictions become the staple food for our responses.*

Grace and obedience

'Grace and active obedience are complementary. There is no faith without good works, and no good works apart from faith.'

The Cost of Discipleship

There is nothing so sterile as an obedience marked by legalism rather than grace. This kind of obedience counts its virtues and inspires self-righteousness. Obedience characterised by grace is an obedience which is creative and doesn't keep a record of its own achievements. It almost doesn't know itself. It acts because it is motivated by a loving concern that sees the need of the recipient and not the strength of the giver.

MEDITATION: *Great acts of virtue are always more of a surprise to the giver than to the receiver.*

Christ and the world

'The world has known Christ and has turned its back on him, and it is to this world that the church must now prove that Christ is the living Lord.'

Ethics

There was a time in the Western world when the whole culture was basically Christian. That is no longer the case. Christianity is now frequently regarded with cynicism or disdain. There is little point in Christians longing for a return to that past era. The challenge is rather that we need to face the alien nature of our world and seek to rebuild its values with the claims of Christ. In that process, we clearly need to live out those claims ourselves. Our personal lives and the life of the church should be characterised by grace, healing, reconciliation, justice, mercy, freedom and peace.

THOUGHT: *Christ's relevance for the world will only become obvious when he is relevant in our own lives.*

Liberating love

'. . .I must release the other person from every attempt of mine to regulate, coerce and dominate him with my love.'

Life Together

Love can be liberating. It can also be stifling. When it seeks to control the other person and thus keep that person dependent, love is no longer freeing and upbuilding. It becomes counter-productive because the welfare of the other becomes lost to the need of the giver to feel wanted and helpful. True love always enhances the well-being of the other. And central to this well-being is the encouragement towards independence, responsibility and self-determination.

MEDITATION: *Loving regard for the other has as much to do with withholding as it has to do with giving.*

The way for me

'I do not understand your ways, but you know the way for me.'

Prayer from Prison

We know far less about God and his ways than we are inclined to think. At best we only know the edges of his ways. Our constant prayer therefore ought to be, 'Lord, teach me more about yourself and cause your light to shine upon me.' Because we struggle to understand God and his purposes, we also have difficulty in understanding God's purposes for our lives. As a result, we struggle with issues of divine guidance and knowing God's will. One important starting point for guidance is accepting that, if God knows the way for me, he will also take the trouble to make that way clear to me.

THOUGHT: *God's way for me often lies closer at hand than I first thought and is already embryonically patterned into the way I am gifted and orientated.*

Mixed motives

'It is remarkable how I am never quite clear about the motives for any of my decisions. Is that a sign of confusion, of inner dishonesty, or is it a sign that we are guided without our knowledge, or is it both?'

The Way to Freedom

We all wish that our motives related to decision-making would be pure. But they seldom are. It is not that we do not want to do the right thing by God or others. It is more a matter of other things also influencing us: things such as personal security, acceptance, recognition, appreciation, popularity and power all play a part. These things may not be wrong in themselves, but they crowd into the decision-making process and often mix our motives in deciding to go in a particular direction.

PRAYER: *Lord, I acknowledge that many of my motives are mixed. Grant that even where my own issues and concerns crowd in, that which is right might still emerge. Amen.*

May

You have granted me many blessings;
now let me also accept what is hard
from your hand.

Blessings and hardship

'You have granted me many blessings; now let me also accept what is hard from your hand.'

Prayer from Prison

God's way with us is to move us from dependence and immaturity to responsibility. There are no soft options in this journey. We cannot grow into maturity without the pain of growth, the resolution of disappointments, the acceptance of God's chastisements, the suffering of loneliness and rejection and the transformation of self-regard into true servanthood. Having received many blessings from God's hand, we must joyfully accept the difficulties that come our way in order to become transformed into a much greater Christlikeness.

MEDITATION: *Difficulty from the hand of a loving God is but a future blessing in disguise.*

Those deep motivations

'The reasons one gives for an action to others and to one's self are certainly inadequate. One can give a reason for everything. In the last resort, one acts from a level which remains hidden from us. So one can only ask God to judge us and to forgive us.'

The Way to Freedom

We never fully understand ourselves and therefore need to accept the mystery of our own being. Our motivations will therefore never be totally transparent to us. This we need to accept. What should never be acceptable, however, is that we refuse to be open to the judgment of God and others on the value and effectiveness of the actions that flow from our motivations.

THOUGHT: *When we cannot fully understand ourselves, we need to be open to the God who knows all about us and open to others who may give us valuable feedback.*

A future hope

'As far as my own life is concerned, I must say I have plenty to aim at, to do and to hope for to keep me fully absorbed, yet without wanting anything for myself.'

Letters and Papers from Prison

For some people, present difficulty means putting their life into neutral. They plan, hope and dream only when things are well. But no difficulty should stop us from planning, hoping, praying and dreaming. Such an approach would be a waste of our sorrows. Difficulty is often the mother of new hopes and dreams. The genuineness of these hopes and dreams will be marked by the fact that they are not hopes simply for our deliverance from difficulty, but for new possibilities of faith and action.

MEDITATION: *Difficulty is no barrier to faith and hope.*

Our present reward

'You love goodness and reward it on this earth with a clear conscience and, in the world to come, with a crown of righteousness.'

Prayer from Prison

Some people believe that the reward of the righteous in this life involves every kind of material and spiritual blessing. Fortunately, this is not so. Being satiated and self-satisfied is hardly the badge of blessing. It is a far greater blessing that God keeps us empty rather than filled. The greatest reward that God can give us here is not to fill us with good things, but to give us his stamp of approval. Having his approval and benediction means that we can live with a clear conscience.

THOUGHT: *The reward of a clear conscience may not appear to be much at first glance, but it is like a golden seam that gives our life true quality.*

The deluding dazzle of possessions

'Earthly possessions dazzle our eyes and delude us into thinking that they can provide security and freedom from anxiety. Yet all the time they are the very source of all anxiety.'

The Cost of Discipleship

We all need money and resources to live. To have things is certainly no sin, for asceticism is not the mark of spirituality. This mark can only be obedience to Jesus Christ. Yet as followers of Christ we can also be deluded by the power of 'much having'. The grasping after more is often not an expression of the desire to progress, but to increase our power and status. This desire can become an insatiable hunger which cuts across Jesus' call for us to be servants, to hunger for God's kingdom and righteousness, and to look to God to meet our identity needs.

MEDITATION: *Often the things we grasp after as giving us meaning and security are the very things that undermine the fabric of our lives.*

That personal word

'"Do your best to come before winter" (2 Timothy 4: 21). It is not a misuse of scripture if I take that to be said to *me* — if God gives me the grace to do it.'

The Way to Freedom

While scripture tells us how God has acted in the past and how men and women responded, it is also a *present* source of encouragement, inspiration and direction. It encourages us to trust this same God with our struggles and hopes. The Bible's stories, wisdom, instruction, history, songs, poems and ethical teaching can all guide our present actions. Specific words of scripture that somehow strike home can give us personal and specific guidance today. But such a specific word never does away with the need for reflection, faith, trust and prayer.

PRAYER: *Father, grant that your word will be a living word for me that will give my life direction, hope and purpose. Amen.*

Praise and adoration

'. . . we. . . learn again something of the praise and
adoration that is due the triune God at break of day,
God the Father and Creator who has preserved our
life through the dark night and wakened us to a new
day; God the Son and Saviour, who has conquered
death and hell for us and dwells in our midst as victor; God the Holy Spirit, who pours the bright gleam
of God's word into our hearts at the dawn of day,
driving away all darkness and sin and teaching us to
pray aright.'

Life Together

We are much more given to asking than prais-
ing, to questioning than adoration, and to wanting than thanking. And yet we have so much
that should spur us on to praise and adoration,
especially the great gift of faith which has
caused us to see the love of God made manifest
in Christ Jesus. In living daily in the wonder of
God's love and presence, our asking, questioning and wanting cannot but become transformed into praise, adoration and thankfulness.

THOUGHT: *Adoration of Father, Son and Holy Spirit
brings life into a much truer perspective.*

Love for the world

'There can be no genuine love of the world except the love wherewith God loved it in Jesus Christ.'

The Cost of Discipleship

We are to love the world intensely. We are to love and care for its natural beauty. We are to appreciate and enhance the richness of its cultures. And we are to love people whether they are Christian or not. We are not, however, to love the 'worldliness' of the world with its pride and rebellion and its rejection of God's rulership. Our love for the world can only be sustained if we continue to be motivated by the love of Christ shed abroad in our hearts.

MEDITATION: *The love of Christ always draws us towards the world and not away from it.*

New manna for a new day

'I must take care not to be remiss with Bible reading and prayer.'

The Way to Freedom

In engaging the Bible as a conversation partner, we dialogue with none other than God himself. God never expects us to be simply passive listeners, for then we would not learn anything new. It is only as we come with our questions, our seeking, our hunger and our openness that we learn anything new. God is not only happy to speak to us; he is even happy for us to speak to him about our fears, questions, struggles and pain.

THOUGHT: *The Bible and prayer are two avenues for mutual conversation and dialogue.*

Treating the enemy as a brother and sister

'. . .our enemies are those who harbour hostility against us, not those against whom we cherish hostility. . . The Christian must treat his enemy as a brother and requite his hostility with love. His behaviour must be determined not by the way others treat him, but by the treatment he himself receives from Jesus.'

The Cost of Discipleship

There is little virtue in loving someone we have made into an enemy. Far better never to have made him into an enemy in the first place. But where the other unjustly regards us as the enemy, we need to respond with a love that seeks to lessen the other's pain and bitterness. The enemy who hates and retaliates is the person who suffers far more than the one who is the object of his anger. Like Jesus, we, too, need to extend forgiveness to those who wrongfully mistreat us.

PRAYER: *Father, I am usually so quick in reacting to unjust treatment. Help me rather to treat such a one with the same generosity that Christ shows to me. Amen.*

No respecter of persons

'You hate and punish evil without respect of persons in this world and the next.'

Prayer from Prison

As Christians we run the danger of thinking
that we have such a special position with God
that he is happy to condone whatever we do.
We think that we can sin cheaply because
God's grace will be extended to us. But God is
no respecter of persons. God's love and grace
is always matched by his passion for justice.
Rather than thinking that God will treat us
more gently, the opposite is in fact true. He
will discipline us the more strictly because of
his love for us.

THOUGHT: *Mercy and justice, grace and discipline
belong together.*

An enlightened mind

'We pray anew every day, when we open our eyes in the morning and when we close them at night, that God will enlighten the eyes of the heart.'

Meditating on the Word

Insight, inspiration and enlightenment are the things we need to make our lives rich, meaningful and effective. We cannot rely on the obvious, or simply accept what first appears to be the case. We need to penetrate through things to touch the real issues. For this we need the discernment that is particularly appropriate to each area of our lives. As we gain greater spiritual insight, this should help us to gain a better perspective on ourselves, on others, on the human condition and on life's purpose.

MEDITATION: *Insight is a gift that comes for those who hunger after truth.*

Realism

'The believer can be neither a pessimist, nor an optimist. To be either is illusory. The believer sees reality not in a certain light, but he sees it as it is and believes only in God and his power towards all and over all that he sees.'

No Rusty Swords

The Christian is called to face life realistically. To be a realist is not to deny the importance of faith and prayer. Nor does it mean that one is hard or sceptical. The realist approaches life responsibly and is not prepared to let 'pie in the sky' dreams determine important life responses. But the realist also looks at life in the light of God's grace, action and involvement. Thus a realist is always a person of faith and hope.

MEDITATION: *We are to look at ourselves and the world with sober judgment, but also with the measure of faith that God has given us.*

Secrets

'. . .there are many things in human life which ought to be kept covered over.'

Letters and Papers from Prison

We frequently talk of the importance of openness, honesty and transparency in relationships. This is particularly appropriate where we have compromised our commitments. At those points we need to be open with our confession. We also need to be open with our plans, hopes and dreams with those with whom we are joined in a common life journey. But there are many things which belong to the sacredness of our own being. These should not be shared, but should be kept as a reservoir from which we draw our nourishment.

THOUGHT: *Openness and closure, giving and keeping form the rhythm of life.*

The greater challenge

'He must from the outset discard as irrelevant the two questions. . . "How can I be good?" and "How can I do good?" and instead of these he must ask the utterly and totally different question, "What is the will of God?"'

Ethics

The concern with the question: 'How can I be good?' is that there is the danger that we will become preoccupied with trying to quantify our own spirituality. Those who are forever taking their own spiritual pulse may never hear what God is actually asking of them. Similarly, a preoccupation with the concern 'how to be good' may get us into methods, programmes and priorities, but may prevent us from taking the risk of hearing God's will. An openness to hear the will of God takes courage and flexibility, for we may well find that we have to take a different direction.

MEDITATION: *In seeking the will of God, I risk everything that is safe and secure about my world. But in doing the will of God, I find an even greater security.*

Truth

'We may not play with the truth, or else it will destroy us.'

No Rusty Swords

Truth is something we are constantly to seek after, embrace and affirm. Yet in seeking truth, it is not so much a matter of us finding the truth, but rather of it finding us. And when it does, we cannot but surrender to it. It is in this surrender that we establish the foundation for a life of integrity. It is in refusing to positively respond to the claims that truth makes on our lives that we discover that truth turns from being a friend to being a foe who condemns us.

PRAYER: *Lord, grant that your light and your truth may shine upon the whole of my life, challenging me to live by its direction. Amen.*

The mark of solitude

'The mark of solitude is silence, as speech is the mark of community.'

Life Together

From the busyness of work, family and church life and from the challenge of our tasks in the world, we need to withdraw for renewal, restoration and affirmation. Withdrawal in itself does not necessarily lead to renewal. We need to unburden ourselves and so become still. In being still we are to become empty. And in our emptiness we can look to God to fill us with new things. That newness may not necessarily be new purposes or new goals. It simply may be coming to a new determination to press on with what needs to be done. It may also be a simple affirmation of who we are and of God's love for us.

THOUGHT: *Silence is not busily talking inside one's own head. It is being open and empty, but expectant of God's light and consolation.*

New possibilities

'The will of God is directed not only to the new creating of men, but also to the new creating of conditions.'

No Rusty Swords

God's agenda has human beings as its major focus. He is concerned that they should experience the transforming power of Christ's love and live their lives accordingly. But God's agenda is also wider. He is concerned about the whole of society, the whole world and the world which is to come. Clearly our concerns should also stretch beyond the personal, the family and the church. If God's love is for the whole world, then we should work for change in the whole of our society. But real change can only come when God opens up new possibilities and we are willing to respond appropriately.

MEDITATION: *New conditions can be significant in producing new men and women, and new men and women can help to create new conditions.*

Begin with me

'All repentance and renewal must begin with me. . .
Looking upon the evil-doing of others does not help
me, and it helps me just as little to marvel at the
righteousness of others.'

Meditating on the Word

It is easy to compare ourselves with other
people; we are often quick to see the faults of
others and where they should change. But
change cannot start with the other person; it
must begin with me. It is when *I* change in my
attitudes and my actions that I am blessed with
the moral power to influence others for good.
Power comes not by placing demands on
others, but by being transformed ourselves into
the likeness of Christ.

THOUGHT: *One of the greatest forms of blindness is
to be unaware of our own faults and weaknesses.*

Lost time

'Time lost is time when we have not lived a full human life — time unenriched by experience, creative endeavour, enjoyment and suffering.'

Letters and Papers from Prison

We cannot only measure our lives on the basis of busyness and productivity. It must also be measured on the basis of quality and creativity. And more particularly, it should be measured in the light of our seeking to fulfil what God has asked of us. If we seek to live and learn from life and its experiences, then nothing need be lost in gaining a heart of wisdom.

MEDITATION: *Lost time is when we learn nothing from the experiences of life.*

Blessing and conflict

'Which of us has really admitted that God's goodness leads us into a conflict?'

No Rusty Swords

We might think that God's blessings should
always lead us into the way of peace and happiness. But this is not always the case. God's
blessings can also be the preparation for battle,
the strength for the fight, the provision for the
difficult journey, the enabling for the challenge,
the power to face the enemy and the grace to
resist the temptation.

PRAYER: *Lord, I expected peace, but instead the battle rages. Help me to change my expectation of
what ought to be so that I can face reality without
bitterness or fear, but with the hope that you will see
me through. Amen.*

Carrying the cross

'The cross is laid on every Christian. The first
Christ-suffering which every man must experience
is the call to abandon the attachments of this world.'
The Cost of Discipleship

Carrying one's cross has nothing to do with a
servile submission to difficulty or disaster. Instead, it has everything to do with a joyful
abandonment to doing the will of Christ. Ful-
filling Christ's will always involves putting the
concerns of God's kingdom before the pursuit
of our own security, possessions, status and
power.

MEDITATION: *The cross calls into account every
security that is not based on the security of abandonment to Christ.*

True friendship

'Thus the very hour of disillusionment with my brother becomes incomparably salutary, because it so thoroughly teaches me that neither of us can live by our own words and deeds, but only by that one word and deed which really binds us together — the forgiveness of sins in Jesus Christ.'

Life Together

Fellowship and friendship cannot be based on our ability to live up to each other's expectations. For not only are our expectations of others too great, but our ability to perform is often too weak. Rather, true fellowship and friendship continues to find its inspiration in the commitment to love irrespective of the other's performance, and in the willingness to forgive each other's failures and sins.

MEDITATION: *Love can continue in spite of the failure of the other and the weakness of my own love, for both can be renewed by the grace of God.*

The value of the human being

'The real man is not an object either for contempt or for deification, but an object of the love of God.'

Ethics

We are not nothing. Nor are we God. We have significance, but we are fallen. We are capable of great good as well as horrendous evil. We are frequently contradictory, but we are also capable of consistency and single-mindedness. But none of these things adequately describes who we really are. What does describe us is that we are made in God's image, and are loved by God and enabled by him to live life in faith, trust and obedience.

THOUGHT: *Our self-identity comes from being loved by a personal God who declares us valuable and significant.*

Resisting evil

'The fanatic imagines that his moral purity will prove a match for the power of evil but, like a bull, he goes for the red rag instead of the man who carries it, grows weary and succumbs.'

Letters and Papers from Prison

In resisting evil, we can never assume that it will simply go away because we are virtuous and moral. Nor should we confuse a particular manifestation of evil with its source. In making both mistakes, we either fail to take action or fight the wrong enemy. In failing to take a stand, we lose ourselves and, in fighting the wrong enemy, we act irresponsibly. In resisting evil, we need moral courage and discernment.

MEDITATION: *Identifying the real enemy is half the battle.*

Lord of the whole of our life

'Had Levi stayed at his post, Jesus might have been his present help in trouble, but not the Lord of his whole life.'

The Cost of Discipleship

We are quite happy for Jesus to add something to our life. We are less happy for him to take something away. What is even more startling is when the call of Jesus causes a deep rupture in our previous lifestyle and calls us to new priorities and concerns. This reorientation may well shake our previous securities, but can only lead us to a new state of blessedness and growth.

THOUGHT: *If Jesus Christ cannot challenge our lives to adopt new priorities, then he does not touch the central issues of our lives.*

The word of salvation

'If somebody asks him, "Where is your salvation, your righteousness?" he can never point to himself. He points to the Word of God in Jesus Christ, which assures him salvation and righteousness.'

Life Together

Hope and salvation do not lie within us or within our world systems. They lie in the message that Christ, God's Son, has come amongst us and has made the way of reconciliation open through his death and resurrection. That Christ had to come to show us the way is not so much a negative reflection on our value as persons, but an acknowledgement of our need. And for those who acknowledge their need, the knowledge that God has provided for us is good news indeed!

MEDITATION: *It is not a negative reflection on who we are to acknowledge that we need the love and grace of God.*

Reservoir of past knowledge

'But just as the capacity to forget is a gift of grace, so memory, the recalling of the lessons we have learnt, is an essential element in responsible living.'

Letters and Papers from Prison

Over time, in our responses to people and situations, we build up a body of knowledge that can help us to make fruitful judgments in the present. Yet we always need to regard the wisdom of the past as a reservoir rather than as a set of prescriptive rules. Lessons learned from the past are valuable only if they are applied to the present with sensitivity, flexibility and grace.

THOUGHT: *The wisdom that we gain over many years must always be open to further change, relevant application and growth.*

Opportunities for service

'Possessions are not God's blessings and goodness, but the opportunities of service which he entrusts to us.'

No Rusty Swords

What we have we easily regard as our own. We see ourselves as masters rather than stewards. What we have we regard as the result of our own achievements and therefore as our right to possess and claim and hold. But in the final analysis, what we have has been given, for our very life was given and our gifts and talents are equally the result of God's beneficence. So what we have can only provide us with opportunities for stewardship, generosity and sharing.

THOUGHT: *To pass something on to another is not to lose it, but to invest it.*

Simplicity of the good news

'It will always be true that the wisest course for the disciple is always to abide solely by the word of God in all simplicity.'

The Cost of Discipleship

We can make it all very difficult. In fact, we can make the good news obscure. We can make it an object of historical study, or the focus of a philosophical or ethical treatise, rather than a word which addresses us and challenges us to believe its precepts and to live accordingly. What is difficult about the Bible is not so much in understanding it, but in living it out.

THOUGHT: *The disciple wants to hear the word of the Master. And because he loves the Master and is loved by him, he finds the Master's words believable and liveable.*

The gentle and easy yoke

'What is a gentle and easy yoke when done in obedience becomes an insupportable burden when done in disobedience.'

The Way to Freedom

No task that seeks to serve others, whether that be in the home, at work or in the church, is ever easy. This is particularly so when those tasks involve long-term commitments. To be sustained in such commitments requires the knowledge that what we are doing is our responsibility and is appropriate. We can then call on God to help us and to encourage us in the journey. But when our tasks are performed without a sense of God's direction and help, then we walk a difficult and hard road.

THOUGHT: *To seek to serve others without God's direction and sustenance will probably embitter us, for we walk alone and probably will not see the expected fruit of our labour.*

June

We are here and we are joined together not as a community of those who know, but of those who all look for the word of their Lord.

Uncertain certainty

'We are here and we are joined together not as the community of those who know, but of those who all look for the word of their Lord.'

No Rusty Swords

There is much that we can be sure about in the area of faith, but there is always uncertainty in how to live that faith. We always have to wrestle with scripture to make it relevant for our time. So this question is always pressing: 'Lord, what are you saying to me and your people at the moment?' This should never be seen as a problem, but as one way for God to challenge us yet again.

MEDITATION: *Not to be sure opens up new opportunities to search out the truth.*

The struggle of faith

'When all is said and done, the life of faith is nothing if not an unending struggle of the spirit with
every available weapon against the flesh.'

The Cost of Discipleship

We would like our faith in Christ to put to an
end decisively our struggles about meaning
and life direction, and problems with our sin
and wrongdoing. But faith does no such thing.
These struggles continue and often intensify.
Sin and wrongdoing become much more sensitive issues. The issue of meaning remains difficult as we seek to make our faith in Christ
relevant in a flawed world and the matter of
one's life direction becomes all the more pressing.

THOUGHT: *Faith in Christ is as much a struggle as
it is a way of peace.*

Duty is never enough

'When men are confined to the limits of duty, they never risk a daring deed on their own responsibility, which is the only way to score a bull's eye against evil and defeat it. The man of duty will in the end be forced to give the devil his due.'

Letters and Papers from Prison

To be men and women of duty is commendable. But it is dangerous when duty asks us to suppress truth or when it demands loyalties that are idolatrous. Doing our duty is never enough, for God has called us to be creative and responsible and therefore we need to make responses that are beyond the call of duty. To live like that is always risky, but also potentially productive. It may stem a tide of evil or open the floodgates of righteousness.

MEDITATION: *God's call to justice, mercy and peace qualifies every commitment to duty.*

Sorrow bearers

'The disciple-community does not shake off sorrow
as though it were of no concern of its own, but willingly bears it.'

The Cost of Discipleship

Martin Luther translated, 'Blessed are those
who mourn' to mean 'Blessed are those who
are the sorrow-bearers'. As Christians, we not
only have our own sorrows and burdens to
bear, but also those of others. In practice, this
means that we take other people's tragedies
and difficulties to our own hearts in intercessory prayer and in helpful service. In adopting
this ministry, we ourselves will also be com-
forted.

THOUGHT: *Sorrow bearers need not be depressed
persons, but caring persons sustained by the comfort of the Spirit.*

Relevant teaching

'Preaching which has its roots in practical work as well as in the life and experience of the community will be more relevant.'

The Way to Freedom

The more formal roles of teaching and pastoral care in the church should not isolate us from normal life. It is better that those who fill these roles should also have other vocations. Where teaching and preaching come out of normal life experience lived in the light of scripture, and where they spring from a life of Christian fellowship and caring, such teaching can provide the necessary insights into a life of discipleship which is relevant for our world.

THOUGHT: *The priesthood of all believers should involve all in the ministry of the church, and all in the church in involvement in the world.*

Response to God's call

'The responsible man seeks to make his whole life a response to the question and call of God.'

Letters and Papers from Prison

Being sensitive to God's call does not mean forever looking over our shoulder to see what God may want us to do next, while failing to get on with making long-term commitments. God is not fickle, and responding to God's call does not mean that we are forever changing direction. The key response is to make a commitment to be involved in God's redemptive concern for the world whether we are single, married, well-off, poor, technicians or clergy.

PRAYER: *Lord, grant that wherever I may find myself, I make your ministry of liberation, redemption and justice my priority. Amen.*

Like him

'It is only because he became like us that we can become like him. It is only because we are identified with him that we can become like him. By being transformed into his image, we are enabled to model our lives on his.'

The Cost of Discipleship

Jesus not only saves us from our sin and self-concern, but he also draws us into a conformity to his words and ways. This is where salvation becomes costly, for it calls us to model our lives on that of Jesus. This means that we emulate his passion for the Father's will — his concern for reconciliation, healing and freedom — and that we live for the sake of God's kingdom.

MEDITATION: *It is not only what Christ does for us, but more importantly what he does in us that will reflect the cost of discipleship.*

You are there, even when all fail

'You abide with me when all men fail me; you remember and seek me; it is your will that I should know you and turn to you.'

Prayer from Prison

God is not only there when we are alone or in difficulty, for he is always with us in all the circumstances of our lives. But in times of distress, we can appreciate anew that our God is ever watchful, faithful and a present help in time of trouble. Though he will especially seek us out, we also need to turn to him in faith and trust.

THOUGHT: *God's watchful presence is appreciated anew when we most need him.*

Living the Christian life

'It is becoming clearer every day that the most urgent problem besetting our church is this: How can we live the Christian life in the modern world?'

The Cost of Discipleship

Some people think that the most urgent question is, 'How can we *proclaim* the Christian faith in our world?' While that is important, there is a more pressing issue — *living* the Christian life. Proclamation that is not backed up by lifestyle is practically useless. Authentically living the Christian life cannot mean living in an ecclesiastical ghetto, but in the midst of life with all its pressing issues. It means that we are to seek God's mind on the meaning-issues of life as well as that of politics and economics. It also means that we need to work out appropriate strategies for our involvement.

MEDITATION: *Deeds are stronger than words and lifestyle must undergird our proclamation to give it meaning and integrity.*

Larger than life

'Peter. . . is nothing but a man confessing his faith.'
No Rusty Swords

It doesn't take much for us to idealise people, making them larger than life. We do this particularly with the past heroes of faith. But they, too, were like us. It is not on Peter that God promises that he will build his church, but on Peter the believer in Jesus Christ. It is not our greatness that will further the kingdom of God, but our daring to believe the claims of Jesus and to take them seriously for the way we live.

THOUGHT: *Greatness is always limited by the eye of the beholder, while faith in God's provision in Christ knows no limits.*

God's watchful eye

'In my sleep he watches yearning
and restores my soul,
So that each recurring morning, love
and goodness make me whole.'

Prayer from Prison

Everything good does not result from our own willing and doing, even when that willing and doing is concerned with the will of God. The good that we may do first of all comes from what is given to us. And much that is given we haven't even asked for. God is constantly renewing and sustaining us. Even while we sleep, he restores our soul.

MEDITATION: *Greater is the quiet Giver who gives unexpectedly, than we are in our appropriating that which is given.*

Standing our ground

'Who stands his ground? Only the man whose ultimate criterion is not in his reason, his principles, his conscience, his freedom or his virtue, but who is ready to sacrifice all these things when he is called to obedient and responsible action in faith and exclusive allegiance to God.'

Letters and Papers from Prison

Our ideas, priorities, philosophies and values may be very important to us, but they can never be the ultimate ideals by which we live. Our ideas and values always need to be corrected by scripture and our priorities are always to be subject to the will of God. The person who stands his ground can stand no more securely than on the will of God, and the person who acts can do so no more certainly than in faith and obedience.

PRAYER: *Lord, grant that above all else I may not do what is convenient, or even what seems appropriate, but help me to seek and do your will. Amen.*

Strength in suffering

'Sorrow cannot tire them or wear them down; it cannot embitter them or cause them to break under the strain; far from it, for they bear their sorrow in the strength of him who bears them up, who bore the whole suffering of the world upon the cross.'

The Cost of Discipleship

Sorrow and difficulty cannot destroy us. But if we have no resources with which to handle difficulties, we will be overcome. We will give way to self-pity or despair. The greatest resource with which to respond to sorrow and difficulty is to gain strength from the suffering servant who bore our suffering and sin to win us redemption and freedom.

THOUGHT: *Christ's resources are available particularly for those who bear the sorrows and difficulties of others.*

A tame Christianity

'. . .like a farmer who needs a horse for his fields, he leaves the fiery stallion on one side and buys the tame, broken-in horse. This is just the way men have tamed for themselves a usable Christianity.'

No Rusty Swords

Being a Christian is not just a matter of being kind and patient. It is also a matter of being tough, committed and passionate. This is particularly necessary when things desperately need to change. And things usually do not change when people are only kind and patient, but when, along with such qualities, they are prepared to make the hard decisions no matter what the personal cost, and when they care enough to risk change. There are times when the broken-in horse may be of good use, but sometimes we do need the fiery stallion.

MEDITATION: *To be tough and committed is not in conflict with the spirituality that Jesus taught.*

Practical spirituality

'. . .man's entire spirituality is interwoven with
sociality.'

Sanctorum Communio

Christian spirituality is not only that of the
closet, the retreat and the inner life. It is also
that of the overt action, the practical commitment and the public arena. In Christ, heaven
and earth, the secular and the spiritual, and
prayer and action come together. The challenge in this remarkable unity is that we need
to make sure that the social realities of family,
institutional care, church and state partake of
Christ's vision of life and are not allowed to
function as if they are self-existent.

THOUGHT: *Often social realities are seen as being
irrelevant to our spirituality. This results in large
areas of our lives failing to come under the influence
of Christ.*

Self-discipline

'If you would find freedom, learn above all to discipline your senses and your soul.'

Letters and Papers from Prison

Freedom does not mean the ability to do whatever comes spontaneously into one's mind. This could lead to confusion and a lot of wasted energy. Freedom is rather the ability to do what one must. To achieve this, self-discipline is necessary and this always involves saying No to the things that so easily charm and entice us.

MEDITATION: *Discipline is not so much the way by which we are constrained, but the way we channel our energy in a particular direction.*

The masquerade of evil

'The evil one is the most passionate disciple of the good — until he betrays him.'

The Way to Freedom

IF evil always initially appeared in its final state, it would be discernible and obvious. But frequently evil, particularly at its point of genesis, appears to be a friend of the good. It is only much later that its true identity becomes obvious. The need to resist evil at the point of its exposure is almost self-evident. The challenge, however, is to resist evil at its very beginning before it leads to destruction and death. To have this sensitive discernment calls for the help of the Holy Spirit, a mind based on God's truth and an ability to know the critical issues of the times in which we live.

THOUGHT: *We cannot always wait until evil fully reveals itself in order to be sure that it is evil. We also need to risk a judgment that what may appear as good is the beginning of evil.*

Partakers of our prayers

'God's name, God's kingdom, God's will must be the primary object of Christian prayer. Of course it is not as if God needed our prayers, but they are the means by which the disciples become partakers in the heavenly treasure for which they pray.'

The Cost of Discipleship

If all we ever pray for is what we need or want, we are shaping ourselves to become narrow and selfish. If we pray for the things of God's kingdom, we will also be drawn into the concerns and realities of that kingdom. Thus our lives will begin to reflect these new values. Change the focus and concern of our prayers, and our values and lifestyle will also begin to change.

MEDITATION: *Prayer does not change God; it changes us.*

Knowing and obeying

'He who questions the commandment of God before obeying has already denied him.'

No Rusty Swords

There is a lot that needs to be questioned in our world. The philosophers, politicians and experts of our age should be critically evaluated. Sermons and our theologies also need to be questioned. But God's commandments can only be obeyed. This is not to say that they should be obeyed without being understood, but rather that his commandments are best understood when they are obeyed.

THOUGHT: *It is not so much a matter of knowing and then doing, but rather a matter of doing and hence coming to know more fully.*

As God has done to us

'My real relation to the other man is oriented on my relation to God.'

Sanctorum Communio

God's love, mercy, forgiveness and challenge to me is the basis for the way that I relate to other people. To be loved by God means not only loving him in return; it also means finding the purpose for my own being in that love. From this growing wholeness I can relate to others in ways that are positive, freeing and empowering.

MEDITATION: *As one who is loved, I am given the capacity to love others.*

The city of God

'No visible city of God is created in this world.'

No Rusty Swords

We wish that what we do or say will have ultimate significance. We hope that the structures that we create will retain their pristine influence. It is not unfortunate that they do not. Not only do the things that we make change and deteriorate, but they also become irrelevant. It would be sad if we held as ultimate something that is really irrelevant. Our structures are therefore at best transitory and need to be corrected or changed. In this, we have no abiding city here, but long for the ultimate reality in the coming kingdom of God.

THOUGHT: *We need to work hard to do our best with God's blessing, but finally our best will always need correction and change.*

Harmony

'Only in the conflict of wills does genuine life arise.'
Sanctorum Communio

God's quality of life will not emerge amongst us if we are committed to a stifling uniformity. God wills diversity, and human experience evidences a conflict of wills, ideas and purposes. But out of that diversity harmony can emerge as people find a common, God-directed purpose. Harmony won out of diversity will always be richer and more life-giving than a predictable conformity.

THOUGHT: *Those who with a strength of will assert themselves and yet find harmony are the people who will creatively affect our world.*

Readiness for responsibility

'We have learnt a bit too late in the day that action springs not from thought, but from a readiness for responsibility.'

Letters and Papers from Prison

It is possible to know a lot and to be full of good ideas, but this does not necessarily result in purposeful action. Such action only comes when we are willing to assume responsibility for our part in the sins and needs of our family, community, church and world. If we are prepared to admit that we, and not simply others, make a negative contribution, then repentance can prepare us for positive action and real responsibility.

MEDITATION: *Purposeful action comes from a decision to do what needs to be done, despite the cost to myself.*

To the least

'He who offers a cup of cold water to the weakest and poorest who bears no honourable name has ministered to Christ himself, and Jesus Christ will be his reward.'

The Cost of Discipleship

Those who minister to others in the name of Christ will be blessed. But that blessing does not necessarily mean anything other than a fuller possession of the life of Christ. We seldom get back in kind, but that should never be a problem for us. It only becomes a problem if we have not given only for the sake of Christ.

MEDITATION: *Giving for the sake of Christ means that we expect nothing from those to whom we give, but everything from him whose grace and blessing we seek.*

Thirsting for the word

'Anyone who is thirsty will drink water from any utensil, even if it is somewhat inconvenient. . . Anyone who is thirsty has always found living water in the Bible itself or in a sermon *in fact* based on the Bible, even if it were a little out-of-date.'

No Rusty Swords

God's truth is like bread to the hungry and like water for the thirsty. God's word is a light for those who walk in darkness, bringing healing and hope to those who are sick or in despair. It is revealed to those who are seeking and guides those who wish to walk in God's ways. God's truth is not for those who know it all, who are self-satisfied and who are curious, but do not want to be changed. From such the word is hidden, for its meaning only comes to those who willingly obey.

THOUGHT: *Only the satiated leave good food to go to waste, while the hungry rejoice in every good gift.*

Bitter sweet

'Joy is rich in fears; sorrow has its sweetness.'

Prayer from Prison

Life has its mixed blessings. The good pushed to extremity can become ugly, and that which is evil can redemptively be turned to become a blessing in disguise. Pain and suffering can have their productive outcome, and joy and ecstasy can have tinges of sadness and despair. While we never experience things in an un-adulterated purity, this does not mean that life cannot be meaningful, even though it is often bitter sweet.

MEDITATION: *If we don't want a uniform same-ness, then complexity and even contradiction are the remaining options.*

Avoiding the dream world

'By sheer grace, God will not permit us to live even
for a brief period in a dream world.'

Life Together

There is nothing wrong with dreaming, but we
also need to live in the real world. Christians in
particular can wish for a perfect fellowship and
a meaningful community life with fellow
Christians.   But such a fellowship is also
marked by sin.   Such a fellowship also has its
disappointments, favouritism, manipulation
and selfishness.   These things will challenge us
to face the real issues.   However, they need not
destroy the community if repentance is also a
mark of its life.

THOUGHT: *It is finally always more difficult to
maintain a life that avoids real issues, than one
which faces them.*

Grateful remembering

'Remembering becomes a power in the present because the God who once acted for me is the living God who today makes me sure of what he has done.'

Meditating on the Word

We don't worship a God who is a past memory, but the Lord who has acted in many and wonderful ways in the past and who also acts in our present. While the Exodus, the giving of the law at Sinai, the fall of Jericho, the amazing events surrounding Jesus' birth and the coming of the Spirit at Pentecost appear to be far more dramatic than the way God acts today, we should never forget God's gracious acts in our time. The miracle of a powerful Christian presence in developing countries despite the negative legacy of Western colonialism, and the significant Christian movements within the virtually defunct communist block demonstrate that God is building his church. The issue is not so much how God worked in the past; we need eyes to see how he is working in our world.

Matthew 6: 1-4   **June 29**

Just doing it

'We are again asking about good works instead of doing this work ourselves in such a way that the left hand does not know what the right hand is doing.'

The Way to Freedom

We can speculate much about how we can act meaningfully and purposefully in our world. But finally we need to do what lies right at hand. If we are open to grasp the opportunities that come our way, we will have ample things to do. This does not mean that we act haphazardly and there may be things that we need to say No to, but we cannot fail to do what clearly must be done.

MEDITATION: *Giving, expecting nothing in return, is a state of being that can only be graced by God's Spirit.*

The true leader

'The true leader must always be able to disillusion.'
No Rusty Swords

The good leader needs to work hard at strategising, mobilising and inspiring. But the leader also needs to help people gain a more realistic picture of his role and abilities. A leader who feeds his ego on the larger-than-life adulation of his followers is a danger to himself and to others. A leader needs to delegate, acknowledge weakness and disbelieve other people's myths about him. Moreover, he needs to see his position as a privileged responsibility and not as an inherent right.

MEDITATION: *The good leader has a true perspective on his position, role and tasks as well as his responsibility and his shortcomings.*

July

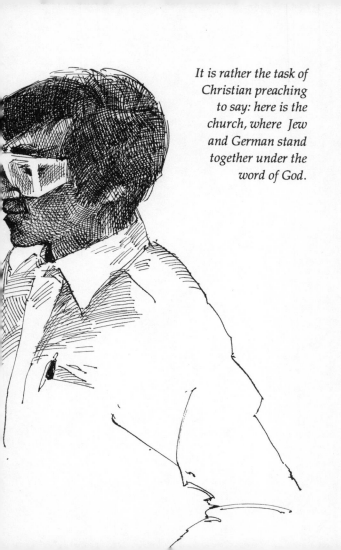

It is rather the task of Christian preaching to say: here is the church, where Jew and German stand together under the word of God.

One in Christ

'It is rather the task of Christian preaching to say:
here is the church, where Jew and German stand
together under the word of God.'

No Rusty Swords

We seem to be better at identifying those who
are not a part of us rather than including those
who should be a part of the family of God. We
seem to be good at making distinctions between ourselves and others — Catholics and
Protestants, evangelicals and charismatics,
liberationists and conservatives — with the im-
plication that we are better than the others. Yet
finally it does not matter so much what ecclesiastical labels we wear. The central issue is
whether we are responding to what God says
in truth, love and unity.

THOUGHT: *Our distinctions are seldom acknowledged by God.*

Sin and its consequences

'Every act [of sinning] is at once an individual act, and one in which mankind's general sin is brought to life again.'

Sanctorum Communio

Sin is not some inevitable subterranean stream that binds us all together. Rather it is a consequence resulting from individual acts of wrongdoing. Sadly, we never sin without that having consequences for others. In this we are responsible for compounding the evil in our world. And just as an act of goodness can have implications far beyond its own immediate sphere, so an act of evil can have results far beyond its apparent impact. We need only think of how damaging, unsubstantiated gossip can spread like dandelion plumes in the wind. Clearly, we need God's grace to help us to stop at sin's point of genesis.

THOUGHT: *Sin has a way of compounding its effect.*

Thanksgiving and obedience

'Thanks to God which does not proceed from an obedient heart is presumption and falsehood.'

Meditating on the Word

Only the person, who in the way of obedience receives the blessing of God, can be sure that it is indeed a blessing for which he is giving thanks. Much that comes our way may appear to be a blessing, but its long-term outworking shows it to be otherwise. All gifts are not necessarily good gifts and the last thing we need are gifts that come from our own presumption or from the demands we place on God's goodness. Worthwhile blessings and gifts always come from God's free response to our obedience and faith.

THOUGHT: *We can only really thank God for what he freely gives, not what we have demanded.*

Christus is for the world

'Everything would be ruined if one were to try to reserve Christ for the church. . . Christ died for the world.'

Ethics

If Christ is for the world and not simply for the church, then we can expect to find him already active and present in the world. The church so often ties itself in knots trying to find appropriate ways to bring Christ to the world, when in fact it should work where Christ is already present. His presence may be in new social movements, youth idealism, political crises, personal grief, economic difficulty or new movements of hope or peace. Christ's presence in these events is always hidden. The task of the church is to proclaim Christ openly so that women and men may believe in him as the Son of God, the Saviour and the Lord of all of history.

THOUGHT: *We may wish to bring Christ to someone, but usually he is already there, for Christ is the one who goes before us.*

Jesus at the extremities

'He stands in my place, where I should stand and cannot. He stands on the boundary of my existence, beyond my existence, but still for me.'

Christology

Jesus has gone further than I could ever go by dying in my place. His presence in our world is persistent and significant. Women and men continue to respond to his claims, model their lives on his words, acknowledge him as Lord, look to him for empowerment and direction, and worship and serve him. This continuing miracle is due to the fact that, at every point, Jesus is there for us, making a way, encouraging, forgiving, enlightening and renewing.

MEDITATION: *Being for us, Jesus always leads us forward.*

Daily work

'Work becomes a curse where our power over things changes into the power of things over us.'

No Rusty Swords

As vice-regents with God, we are called to shape our world with care, justice and truth. We do this through our responsible actions and daily labour. Our work is to express care for our world and we must not simply exploit it. Moreover, our work must be beneficial to society and not destructive. But though the role of worker is important, work must not control us. Only God's will should finally shape our lives. This means that we will need to be able to say No, change our priorities and relegate work to an appropriate place in our lives.

MEDITATION: *The person who controls his own spirit is mightier than he who rules a city.*

Faith's vision

'Faith means being held captive by the sight of Jesus Christ.'

Ethics

Faith is not simply a commitment to Christian principles, holding an abstract idea about God, or a belief in a holy book. Nor is it a psychological technique whereby we talk ourselves into believing that the greater things are beyond our reach. Faith is rather being captivated by the vision of life portrayed in the words and actions of Jesus. Faith embraces his redemptive love for us. Faith is focussed on Christ going before us, even through death. If faith is to be sustained, it will need to have Christ constantly in focus.

THOUGHT: *Faith is not a right emotion or feeling, but a right focus on him who alone can point us to a better world.*

Better days ahead?

'It is not for us to prophesy the day, but the day will come when men will be called again to utter the word of God with such power as will change and renew the world.'

Letters and Papers from Prison

One of the wonderful things about being a Christian is that we can always live in the hope that the present is not the last word. Things can always change and, at particular times in the life of the church, things have changed radically and dramatically. We can think of the Wesleyan Revival or the dynamism of the church in many developing countries. It is good to remember, particularly when we struggle under the dead weight of formalism, that God is ahead of us and that new opportunities and new blessings will come. But these will only come when we embrace anew the challenging words of Christ.

THOUGHT: *While faithfulness should characterise our present, hope should mark the future.*

The indwelling word

'It is never sufficient simply to have read God's word. It must penetrate deep within us, dwell in us like the Holy of Holies in the Sanctuary, so that we do not sin in thought, word or deed.'

Meditating on the Word

Just knowing scripture does not mean that it will change us or automatically prevent us from doing wrong. Scripture must be believed, must come alive for us as being important and relevant, and must be acted upon if it is to be a power for good in our lives. The power of scripture lies in its ability to give the wanderer direction; the disillusioned, hope; the seeker, answers; the discouraged, comfort; and provide us with the words that reflect God's heart and purpose.

MEDITATION: *God's word must become part of the way we think if it is to direct us.*

I and thou

'Community is between individuals, with no blurring of the boundaries of I and thou.'

No Rusty Swords

Community is never a grey uniformity, but a colourful participation where male and female, rich and poor, able and disabled can find a common but diverse life together in Jesus. Community can be a fellowship that avoids rigid communitarianism on the one hand, and an isolating individualism on the other. It is a fellowship that celebrates harmony rather than conformity, and has a vision of life that is large enough to make room for all who wish to serve God in the world in a variety of ways.

MEDITATION: *The richness of I and thou must be preserved in such a way that difficult harmony is always preferred to easy conformity.*

The past and the future

'The past and the future of his whole life are merged in one in the presence of God. The whole of the past is comprised in the word *forgiveness*. The whole of the future is in safe keeping in the faithfulness of God.'

Ethics

We never simply live the present, for both the events of the past and the expectations of the future influence it. The good things of the past sustain us in the present, and the hope of the things that are yet before us confidently draw us into the future. At the same time, we need to receive healing from those things in the past that were less than good by extending forgiveness to those who have hurt us; and we need to trust God for his faithful participation in the things that are yet to come.

MEDITATION: *Confidence in the God who holds the future and who has redeemed the past makes the present worth living.*

Don't lose what you have

'If we do not give thanks daily for the Christian fellowship in which we have been placed, even where there is no great experience, no discoverable riches, but much weakness, small faith and difficulty; if, on the contrary, we only keep complaining to God that everything is so paltry. . . then we hinder God from letting our fellowship grow.'

Life Together

We can soon tire of what we have in our life together as Christians, for our expectations usually far exceed the reality. We can thus become ungrateful and complaining. However, this does not mean that we must accept every mediocrity in the church. We should work for change and improvement, but we will only do this effectively if we are thankful for the good that is already there.

THOUGHT: *To be thankful for what we have does not mean that we are blind to what ought to be.*

Life's direction

'From Christ alone must we know what we should do.'

No Rusty Swords

There are times where we may receive a very specific instruction from Christ through his Spirit about what we are to do. At other times we appear to be left to work out specific directions for ourselves. But this does not mean that in having to do this we don't hear from Christ. For if Christ has captivated our heart and we desire to please him above all else, then the struggles that we may experience in coming to particular decisions will not be without Christ's guiding influence.

PRAYER: *Lord, grant that in every decision that I make, I may look for your direction and encouragement. Amen.*

Don't argue with the devil

'We should never argue with the devil about our sins, but we should speak about our sins only with Jesus.'

Temptation

Our sins and failings cannot be rationalised to ourselves or to our accuser, the devil. This will only deepen our guilt and lead to frustration or despair. Sins need to be brought to Jesus for his forgiveness and empowering so that, freed from guilt and shame, we can continue to live in faith, hope and trust.

PRAYER: *Lord, grant that I may never excuse my sin or condemn myself for my wrongdoing, but may I turn to you in repentance and confession. Amen.*

Exploitation

'He forgot that submissiveness and self-sacrifice
could be exploited for evil ends.'

Letters and Papers from Prison

It is never simply enough to be good. It is also
necessary to evaluate to what ends our good is
being used. Children can exploit the kindness
of their parents, and the church and the state
can reward the well-meaning but conforming
members, while excluding those of independ-
ent mind and viewpoint. In giving ourselves to
any cause, we must assume responsibility not
only for our own personal goodwill, but also
for the corporate outcomes.

THOUGHT: *The well-meaning can contribute to
wrong ends if they are not discerning about the way
their service is being used.*

Thinking God's thoughts after him

'We are more fond of our own thoughts than the thoughts of the Bible.'

No Rusty Swords

The thoughts expressed in the Bible are never simply noble. They are also disturbing. They tell us about a holy God and an unrighteous people, a way of life and a way of death, and a way of servanthood instead of a life of selfishness. These thoughts are not there simply to inform us, but more particularly to challenge us to live a life of dedication to the God of whom the Bible speaks.

MEDITATION: *The thoughts of the Bible can be lived out in daily life, but only by the person who follows the way of Christ.*

Concrete responsibility

'It is easier by far to act on abstract principle than
from concrete responsibility.'

Letters and Papers from Prison

The actual situations to which we need to
respond are never quite like the way we would
like them to be. Nor are they quite the way we
have learnt in school or textbook that they
should occur. Actual situations are usually
more complex rather than simple, grey rather
than black or white; they take longer to solve
than first anticipated, and require that we be
adaptable and be prepared to get our hands
dirty. Yet it is precisely a response to the concrete situations that marks us out as followers
of Jesus, for he was the one who elevated the
real needs of people above that of the
ceremonial and religious laws of his day.

THOUGHT: *The doing that responds to real situations is usually a costly doing.*

The word of a friend

'Just as you would not dissect and analyse the word
spoken to you by someone dear to you, but would
accept it just as it was said, so you should accept the
word of scripture and ponder it in your heart as
Mary did. . . that is meditation.'

Meditating on the Word

Scripture can be studied and scrutinised. But
meditating on scripture is not studying it, but
requires a patient and loving *listening*. It is a listening that looks for meaning that will bring
hope for the future, direction for the present,
resolution of the past, cleansing from evil, fortitude for difficulty, patience in the face of
meaninglessness and a transformation of the
best that we may have to offer into the greater
good of the purposes of God.

THOUGHT: *The word of a friend should be carefully
thought about and gratefully accepted.*

My concrete existence

'. . .the person in his concrete life, wholeness and uniqueness is willed by God as the ultimate unity.'

Sanctorum Communio

God is practically, not theoretically concerned about us. He does not call us to an ideal, but to a concrete life of obedience. He does not only love me as part of the people of God, but also as an individual. He does not call me to do general good, but to do specific acts of kindness and service. His love for me is not only focussed on spiritual concerns, but embraces the whole of my concrete existence.

MEDITATION: *God's manifold purpose is expressed through the uniqueness and creativity of his many sons and daughters in the faith.*

The way of peace

'There is no way to peace along the way of safety.
For peace must be dared. It is the great venture. It
can never be safe.'

No Rusty Swords

To work for peace in our world frequently
means adopting strategies that are daring and
dangerous, for peace must be won in the face of
those who perpetrate war and aggression.
Peace does not come from those who long for
peace at any price. It comes from those who
dare to risk everything in order that a more
peaceful and just world may begin to emerge.

THOUGHT: *The way of peace is not the way of ac-
quiescence, but of active resistance in the face of evil.*

Destroying the fellowship

'Just as the Christian should not be constantly feeling his spiritual pulse, so, too, the Christian community has not been given to us by God for us to be constantly taking its temperature.'

Life Together

Neither the world nor the devil destroys Christian fellowship; we do. We are often the fifth column that destroys the city. One way in which we undermine the fellowship is by being so self-reflective that we lose our vision of Christ and the nature of our task in the world. An over-preoccupation with the quality of our life together will finally cause us to despise the very things we have, for we will tend to so guard that life together that we choke it. What we have together should be held with an open hand that serves the world, rather than with the closed grasp that finally loses the very thing it seeks to hold.

THOUGHT: *When our life together ceases to be a gift for which we thank God, we become the protectors and eventually the destroyers of the very thing that we cannot keep safe. For what we have can only continue to be given by God and appreciated by us.*

The suffering of the righteous

'That the righteous man suffers on account of his sin is understandable, but that the righteous man suffers for the sake of righteousness — that can easily lead him to the stumbling-block in Jesus Christ.'

Temptation

To suffer for what we didn't do is never easy. It is hard enough for us to be prepared to own responsibility for the wrong we ourselves have done. But to suffer for our commitment to Christ is all the more difficult, for we expect Christ to protect us and not to expose us to harm, danger or opposition. But if we live in the light of God's truth, then opposition, rejection and misunderstanding will inevitably be our lot. This is made all the more difficult when the opposition comes from those whom we thought were our allies and friends.

THOUGHT: *Christ died in the midst of friends who became his enemies.*

Facing my true self

'If my sinfulness appears to me to be in any way smaller or less detestable in comparison with the sins of others, I am still not recognising my sinfulness at all.'

Life Together

We are generally good at seeing other people's faults while failing to recognise our own. But even when we do acknowledge our own shortcomings, we tend to weight them differently than we would the failings of others. For our own faults we make skilful rationalisations, while for the sins of others we often make quick judgments. In doing this, we only expose the sinfulness of our own hearts.

MEDITATION: *The secret of a life of integrity is never to excuse myself, but frequently to excuse the actions of others.*

What we have in Christ

'When a man encounters Christ, everything that Christ is and has is made the property of this man.'

Ethics

Receiving all that Christ has for us is gaining a new life that is disturbing, life-changing and encouraging. It involves blessing and discipleship, hope and suffering, empowerment and humility, strength and confession, and struggle and peace. It is receiving the benefits of Christ's death on our behalf, while at the same time entering a life of discipleship that calls us to walk in the footsteps of the Man from Galilee.

THOUGHT: *Participating in the life of Christ can only be a bitter-sweet experience.*

God, the great initiator

'If we ask how we should begin life with God, the scripture answers that God has long since begun life with us. If we ask what we can do for God, we hear what God has done for us. If we ask how we can live without sin before God, the forgiveness of all sins in Jesus Christ is announced to us.'

Meditating on the Word

We don't begin with God; he begins with us. Before we seek him he is already at work in our lives. He is the one who acts first and what we do is a response to his prompting and love. We are often not aware that God is ahead of us in this way. It is usually in retrospect that we make this discovery. This can only cause us to be thankful, for God was there with us even when we did not know it.

THOUGHT: *True commitment is to be there and available even when that is not expected or initially appreciated.*

The command to love

'The object of Jesus' command is always the same:
to evoke wholehearted faith, to make us love God
and our neighbour with all our heart and soul.'

The Cost of Discipleship

If only we can love, we can perform the
greatest possible service to the other. But love
always needs to find a way and appropriate
means to express itself. These appropriate
means cannot be based on what we think may
be best for the other person. They need to be
based on what is genuinely good for the other.
Love therefore needs to listen before it speaks
and discerning before it acts.

MEDITATION: *The commandment to love is not
meant to stifle our creativity, but to give it a positive
direction.*

Guided by the Spirit

'The community is the body of Christ in which every single member is guided by his Spirit.'
The Way to Freedom

The Christian community does not first of all consist of particular structures. These structures will always change because of differing social, cultural and economic demands. Instead, the community consists fundamentally of those who share a common faith in Jesus Christ and who experience the guidance of the Holy Spirit in their lives. When each member is led by the Spirit, this will mean both unity and diversity, but never uniformity. Thus Christian fellowship will always be characterised by tension and the struggle to find harmony.

THOUGHT: *The harmony that comes out of the common struggle to find a meaningful fellowship will always be at the cost of a certain amount of pain.*

The Accuser and scripture

'The devil. . . takes the word of God's grace in his hand and whispers to us: God is a God of grace; he will not take our sins so seriously.'

Temptation

Scripture is never the sole possession of the Christian. It is also used by the scholar, the sceptic and the Accuser. While the scholar may enrich our understanding of scripture, the sceptic and the Accuser help to undermine our faith in God's truth. And while the sceptic may openly reject the scriptures, the Accuser always uses it sympathetically but destructively — by posing those questions which call God's integrity into question.

MEDITATION: *God's character is no different from his word.*

Individual responsibility

'The individual is responsible before God.'
No Rusty Swords

Finally, we cannot be carried spiritually by the church, husband or wife, pastor or friend. We are responsible before God for our own life, for the choices we make and the way we use our gifts and talents. This is an awesome responsibility. But we never need be alone in exercising our responsibility. The nature of true friendship means that we can be encouraged by our friends to realise our potential through using our gifts and abilities in ways that honour God's call upon our lives.

THOUGHT: *Individual responsibility and corporate encouragement belong together.*

Strength through suffering

'All suffering must lead the Christian to the strengthening of his faith and not to defection.'

Temptation

While we may wish that it was otherwise, suffering is an integral part of life. Suffering can sour us or it can help us to grow. Suffering sours us when we become overwhelmed and lose God's love and encouragement in the situation. It can help us to grow when we make positive responses to our difficulties. Suffering resulting from our own wrongdoing calls us to repent; suffering resulting from the wrongdoing of others calls us to forgive; and suffering that comes from God's hand of discipline challenges us to learn the lessons he wishes to teach us.

THOUGHT: *Suffering only becomes disastrous when we fail to learn its growth-producing lessons.*

Joyful love

'See how joyfully the lover stakes his possessions, his happiness, his honour and life for his loved one . . . and see how miserably our deeds and thoughts for God's love are. . .'

No Rusty Swords

Our love for God often consists of the leftovers that we give to him, when in fact he is deserving of our highest commitment and our deepest motivations. Our love for God, therefore, needs to be constantly renewed. Its renewal cannot depend on some vague guilt feeling that we should be doing better. It can only come from a thankful response to the experience of God's love for us.

MEDITATION: *Great love can only come as a response to being greatly loved.*

August

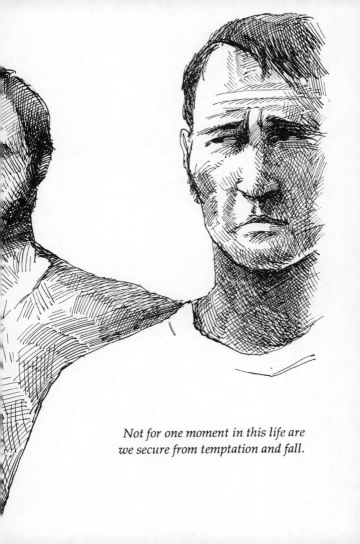

*Not for one moment in this life are
we secure from temptation and fall.*

Temptation and fall

'Not for one moment in this life are we secure from
temptation and fall.'

Temptation

We all like to think that we can be faithful in
our Christian walk and that God will keep us
safe from all harm and temptation. Such is not
the case. We all have our points of vulnerability where the Tempter can penetrate,
and we all run the danger of ceasing to remain
vigilant in our Christian walk. Both weakness
and smugness can be our undoing. So we cannot assume that all is well with us. We can
only continue to live in faith and obedience to
God's call.

PRAYER: *Lord, help me to live in a daily dependence on your grace and empowering, and grant that
I may live in true obedience and faith. Amen.*

The faithfulness of God

'. . .faith stakes everything on the faithfulness of God.'

No Rusty Swords

Faith cannot depend on faith. The exercise of faith cannot depend on our ability to keep on believing. Faith is always our response to the love and faithfulness of God. Thus faith is a gift, since it does not so much lie in us, but is evoked when God's grace and love touches our lives. Even for faith's continuance, we need to trust the faithfulness of God.

THOUGHT: *Relying on God's faithfulness does not relegate us to a life of dependence, but to a life of hopefulness and trust in the God who encourages us to face life responsibly and with courage.*

The start to a new day

'Every day in which I do not penetrate more deeply into the knowledge of God's word in holy scripture is a lost day for me. I can only move forward with certainty upon the firm ground of the word of God.'
Meditating on the Word

The Christian longs to hear God's word. For that word embodies the mind and concerns of a God whom we cannot see, but whom we have encountered by faith. That word is not only a textbook for Christian living, but reveals the nature and character of the God of grace. Like a letter which is a glimpse into the heart of an absent friend, so the Bible reveals a God who has loved us at the cost of the death of his Son. The disclosure of such a love calls us to a persistent intimacy with this Lover.

THOUGHT: *One can get to know the absent other through his words.*

God at the centre

'I should like to speak of God not at the borders of life but at its centre, not in weakness but in strength, not, therefore, in man's suffering and death but in his life and prosperity.'

Letters and Papers from Prison

God is not only there at the point of difficulty and distress, nor is he simply the rescuer and helper in times of emergency. He is also with us in the midst of stability and success. Thus God does not come on the scene only when we need him; he is there all the time — particularly when we think we do not need him. For in our times of well-being and success we need him all the more.

MEDITATION: *We not only need God to do things for us; we also need him just to be there.*

Remaining true

'We shall only be free from care if we remain in the truth that we know, and allow ourselves to be guided only by that. But we stare at the waves, instead of looking to the Lord, and so we are lost.'

The Way to Freedom

The certainties we have regarding our faith and life-direction can easily be undermined. Doubt, the cares of life and disappointments can so perniciously affect us that we begin to lose our way. In finding our way again, it is not so much a matter of discovering new answers, but of remaking old commitments. This has to do with refocussing our gaze on Christ who gave us our faith, hope and life-direction in the first place.

THOUGHT: *Remaining faithful to what we know, when that appears to be undermined, can only be resolved in the rediscovery of that which inspired us in the first place.*

Christ and his church

'Christ's relation to the church is twofold: he is the creator of its whole life, which rests on him, the master-builder of the church; and he is also really present at all times in his church, for the church is his body.'

Sanctorum Communio

The church can be a very exciting place to be. It can also be a boring and moribund institution. Its state of health and dynamism finally depend on whether the church as the people of God truly relies on Christ to sustain all of its life, and whether it seeks the presence of Christ to bless, guide and challenge every aspect of its corporate nature and activities. Where the church loses the sense that it can only exist in and for Christ, its life will ebb away into a conformism that will leave it irrelevant or disillusioned.

THOUGHT: *A people that has its beginnings in the life of Christ must constantly be sustained and renewed by that life.*

In the face of tragedy

'Human and natural catastrophes put our wisdom to silence.'

No Rusty Swords

Tragic, irrational and unexplainable events occur in our world. Such events can also happen to us. When they do, our meaning-system may collapse, our faith may be undermined and our security severely threatened. But such great difficulty need not be the final word, even though it highlights that our previous understandings and explanations of life probably were inadequate. The final word, which drives us to silence and amazement, can always be that out of the ash-heap of tragedy, not only good will come, but a whole new way of understanding life as well.

THOUGHT: *The person who has suffered and yet continues to live in faith and hope is the one whose view on life is worth considering.*

Silence and attentiveness

'To be silent does not mean to be inactive; rather it means to breathe in the will of God, to listen attentively and be ready to obey.'

Meditating on the Word

Speaking is seldom one of our problems; listening is. Action and busyness are usually the norm for our lives; quietness and reflection seldom are. Such reflection is not for the purpose of withdrawal from life. It is the way in which we engage life with a new-found energy and courage. Silence is the mother of speaking. Quietness is the seed-bed for action. Reflection is the impetus for new direction.

THOUGHT: *Silence can lead to solitude and solitude can open to us new possibilities for our restless heart which will lead to an open spirit.*

Temptation and promise

'In the temptation of Jesus, there really remains
nothing except God's word and promise.'

Temptation

In times of difficulty, testing or temptation, we
discover that previous certainties and securities
can quickly evaporate. But being left to feel vulnerable, while probably threatening, is at the
same time an opportunity to open our lives to
God in a new way and to hear his word of
promise afresh.

THOUGHT: *Difficulty, testing and temptation is one
way for us to rediscover where our strength and
security really lie. And since our security does not
lie in what we have achieved or in past experiences,
it can only lie in embracing anew God's word for
our lives.*

All scripture

'But there can be equally little doubt that brief verses cannot and should not take the place of reading the scripture as a whole. . . Holy scripture does not consist of individual passages; it is a unit and is intended to be used as such.'

Life Together

We tend to pick our way through the Bible, grabbing our favourite verses in the same way that children choose their favourite lollies. Like children, we become guilty of maintaining a sweet-tooth diet with all its negative health consequences. We cannot develop a strong spirituality in this way, for we can only grow if we are also challenged and corrected. So those parts of the Bible that we normally don't want to hear also need to become a part of our lives.

MEDITATION: *A one-sided spiritual diet can lead to a superficial satisfaction, but not to growth.*

The great divide

'We cannot unite where God divides.'
No Rusty Swords

While God unites poor and rich, black and white in a community of love and freedom, and will unite heaven and earth in the new reality of the future, there are some things that will never be united. Hatred finally cannot live with love. Sin and righteousness ultimately cannot live together. The will of God cannot be identified with our concerns and God's kingdom is never simply human achievements. So while God is concerned to bring things together, he also separates and divides. While Jesus makes friends and disciples, he also gains enemies. Sadly, it cannot be otherwise, for God's glory and righteousness not only draws people, but it also repels.

MEDITATION: *Unity that is not based on truth is a sham.*

The God of the gaps

'Religious people speak of God when human perception is. . . at an end or human resources fail.'

Letters and Papers from Prison

God cannot simply be pertinent to our lives when we face failure or difficulty. We cannot only invoke him when we have no answers. God is not the God of the gaps when we have run out of human resources or explanations. God is not to be called upon only when human wisdom fails. He is not waiting in the wings to be called upon only when things run into difficulty. He is there at the centre — central to our wisdom, to our answers, to our very life.

THOUGHT: *If we call on God only when we need him, we deny his central place in our lives.*

Where God has acted

'. . .reading of biblical books forces everyone who wants to hear to put himself, or to allow himself to be found, where God has acted once and for all for the salvation of men.'

Life Together

We cannot relive the events of the biblical world, but we can appreciate anew the accounts of God's action in an ancient world and its impact on men and women and their society. In these accounts we cannot find ready-made answers for our world, but we can be inspired by the response of faithful men and women as they sought to honour God and live out the principles of mercy, love and justice in their world.

MEDITATION: *True hearing is always to hear anew. The Bible pressed by new questions will provide us with new answers.*

A temple of the Holy Spirit

'To ruin health deliberately is to destroy one's own soul and God's property.'

No Rusty Swords

To save one's soul but to fail to care for one's body is to give priority to one aspect of who we are at the cost of another. The Bible knows nothing of making the soul the most important aspect of who we are, for it sees the person as a unity. The body, therefore, needs to be cared for as much as the soul. So we need to be gentle with ourselves, finding some balance between work and rest, passion and quietude, activity and celebration.

THOUGHT: *Our body is the way in which our soul, with its great aspirations, can express itself.*

The new community

'The transformation of mankind into a new community is possible only if men are aware of the deficiency of the old.'

Sanctorum Communio

To desire and to work for the new is laudable. But the new never comes into being in pure form. It, too, has its deficiencies and problems. The early church was an alternative to a legalistic Judaism, but it was not without its difficulties and problems. This does not mean that the new should not be attempted. It only means that the new will itself need to be constantly reformed.

MEDITATION: *The new is never totally free from the deficiencies of the old, but the new can be more relevant than the old.*

At the point of temptation

'It is of the very essence of temptation in the Bible that all my strength... is turned against me.'

Temptation

Temptation does not only occur at my point of weakness. If that was so, I could work on strengthening that part of my life. It also occurs at my point of strength, and that is precisely where I can be most vulnerable. In fact, it is my very strength which can be turned against me. For my strength can make me self-satisfied and can blind me to my further needs.

MEDITATION: *Strength can blind me, for it can make me secure in that which can only continually be given through God's bountiful hand.*

Easy on others, hard on ourselves

'I told him in no uncertain terms what I thought of people who can be very hard on others and make grand speeches about living dangerously... and then crumple up themselves under the slightest test of endurance.'

Letters and Papers from Prison

It is easy to be hard on others and gentle on ourselves. We thus place ourselves in a position of strength and power, and run the risk of downgrading the efforts, value and personality of the other person. At the same time, we make ourselves to be better than we in fact are. This approach needs to be reversed. This does not mean that we put other people on pedestals while we downgrade ourselves. Rather, we need to be exacting with ourselves regarding our integrity and motivation, and very generous in ascribing the best of motivations to the actions and efforts of others.

THOUGHT: *We should not have expectations of others regarding things that we are not prepared to carry out ourselves.*

Truthfulness and forgiveness

'Complete truthfulness is only possible where sin has been uncovered and forgiven by Jesus.'
The Cost of Discipleship

No moment of greater honesty is possible than when we open our lives to God in true confession. There we can express, not only our wrongdoings, but also our wrong motivations. There we can confess our sins of omission as well as those of commission. And it is also there that we can rediscover the greatest truth of all, which is not that we are sinful, but that God forgives the sinner who repents.

THOUGHT: *It is a miracle that in the searching light of God's holiness, we are not only exposed, but also loved and forgiven.*

Living without God's word

'The lie of the devil consists of this: that he wishes to make man believe that he can live without God's word.'

Temptation

To be without God's word not only means that we lose the truth and lose our way, but we also lose God himself, for without his word he cannot be known. Sadly, that is not where the down-hill slide ends. For without God's word, we will make the human word authoritative, since we cannot live without someone to guide us. It is always better to struggle to know the seemingly hard word of God, than to know the soothing wisdom of man.

MEDITATION: *God is more than his word, but he cannot be known without his word.*

Stillness and reflection

'God will often require quick action, but he also requires stillness and reflection.'

Meditating on the Word

Reflection is never to be a substitute for meaningful action. For act we must, even when we
know there are risks involved. If we don't act
and respond, then others will act for us and our
lives will be shaped by the determination of
others. But stillness and reflection can make
our actions more purposeful, particularly those
actions which require great commitment and
perseverance. These need to be born out of and
sustained by a certainty that can only come
from having first waited to hear God's voice.

PRAYER: *Lord, help me to wait expectantly, to act
purposefully and to trust you to see me through to
the end. Amen.*

Which kind of good?

'The aim of love is exclusively determined by what
God's will is for the other man.'

Sanctorum Communio

True love seeks to find a way to do a particular
kind of good to the other person — God's
quality of good! And that always has the well-
being of the whole person in view and not
simply immediate blessings and short-term
benefits. God's kind of good always involves
blessing and correction, growth and pruning,
giving as well as withholding. In seeking to do
this kind of good to others, we need to be
prayerful and discerning, so that we do what is
ultimately the best and not what is presently
expedient.

THOUGHT: *Doing for the other person what is
God's will for them calls us to prayer and purposeful action.*

Thou knowest, O God

'Who am I? This or the other? Am I one person today and tomorrow another? Am I both at once? A hypocrite before others, and before myself a contemptibly woebegone weakling? *Who* am I? They mock me, these lonely questions of mine. Whoever I am, thou knowest, O God, I am thine.'

Prayer from Prison

There are times when we struggle anxiously with questions regarding our identity, our purpose and our life-direction. And answers are not forthcoming. At such times we wonder whether God has forsaken us or whether we have lost our way. In these circumstances we may be without answers, but we don't need to be without consolation. Such consolation can only come when we learn to commit ourselves into the hands of God, who doesn't give us answers, but who loves us nonetheless.

MEDITATION: *If I am not sure about who I am and where I am going, I can be sure that God knows all about my uncertainty and, in his time, will show me the way.*

He comes

'Christ comes indeed, and opens up his own way,
no matter whether man is ready beforehand or not.
No-one can hinder his coming, but we can resist his
coming in mercy.'

Ethics

Christ is not waiting in the wings ready to act
when we decide to ask him. He is ever at work,
even when we are not looking for him. And he
is ahead of us, preparing the way and calling us
to follow. We don't determine what Christ is to
do. We are called to participate in his will and
concerns. He does not wait to be invited. He
comes. We simply have to make him welcome.

THOUGHT: *We don't determine whether Christ
comes amongst us. We do, however, play a part in
whether he comes in grace or in judgment.*

Diversity

'But since all persons are created unique, even in the community of love the tension between wills is not abolished.'

Sanctorum Communio

The church should always prefer creative tension to grey uniformity. Our common life in Christ and the unity of the Spirit do not eradicate individuality; they stimulate diversity, for God's work is to make us more truly who we are meant to be. Thus love in the Christian community should, first of all, not be a love based on principle, commonality, doctrinal unity or a common ministry ideology and priority. It should first of all be a love of the individual who is also loved by God. From that starting point, we can attempt to find a unity in the other areas of our life together.

THOUGHT: *Love should not only be extended to those who agree with us, but to all who are loved by God.*

Work in our time

'God has called each one of us to his work in his time.'

No Rusty Swords

We are not simply to be the guardians of the good things that God has done in the past, nor to be simply those who pray for what may happen in the future. We need to be intimately involved in the issues of our time. What these issues are will be identified differently by different members of the Christian church. But however we arrange our priorities for our world, we must include caring for God's creation, encouraging good government, sharing the gospel and promoting justice and righteousness.

THOUGHT: *Different people will see the needs of our world differently. Our concern should not be to get others to accept our agenda, but to do with all our might what we believe we must do.*

God's decisive action in Christ

'In the incarnation we learn of the love of God for his creation; and in the crucifixion we learn of the judgment of God upon all flesh; and in the resurrection we learn of God's will for a new world.'

Ethics

In sending his Son, God does not only demonstrate a concern 'to save souls', but reaffirms his love for the whole of creation and his plan for a new age of righteousness and justice. God's action in Christ is therefore not only for the salvation of men and women, but he also demonstrates his love for the church, the world and all of creation.   Christ is therefore not peripheral to life, with relevance only for an interior spirituality. He is the Lord of all of life, seeking to work his pervasive influence into the fabric of society and the future of the world to come.

MEDITATION: *In Christ, we have the blueprint for the authentic human being, the pattern and relevance of the Christian community, and the basis for a just society.*

Wasted years?

'Yesterday I heard someone say he felt that the last years have been completely wasted as far as he was concerned. I have never felt like that, not even for a moment.'

Letters and Papers from Prison

We have only one life to live. It is this life that needs to be characterised by meaning and purpose. There can be no greater purpose than to live according to God's will. But this does not mean that we will therefore simply enjoy good speed and favourable circumstances. We may, in fact, experience difficulty and struggle. It also does not mean that we will always be productive. Our lives may be lying fallow for a time. Yet both sets of circumstances can be God's will for us. We should be careful that we do not define God's will too narrowly. After all, he is the God who embraces both the time for mourning as well as that of dancing and the time for tearing down as well as that of building up.

PRAYER: *Father, grant that in the varied circumstances of my life I may know your love and participation. Amen.*

The disturbing call of Christ

'We must face up to the truth that the call of Christ does set up a barrier between man and his natural life. But this barrier is no surly contempt for life, no legalistic piety; it is the life which is life indeed, the gospel, the person of Jesus Christ.'

The Cost of Discipleship

Christ is not only the bringer of peace. He is also the great disturber. He does not only bring reconciliation. He also divides. Where men and women respond to his call of discipleship, there is commotion and separation. Family ties may be broken, old allegiances changed and friendships terminated, for nothing can stand in the way of the call of the Master. That call is never the heralding trumpet to some narrow religious and bigoted cause. It is the royal call to be God's servants of righteousness in our world.

THOUGHT: *The call of Christ does not call us away from the concerns of the world. It merely calls us away from selfish allegiances and unproductive priorities.*

Christ the victor

'Christ is risen; he has robbed the devil of his power.'

No Rusty Swords

Jesus the faithful Son of the Father endured that shameful cross and was raised with honour through God's power. His victory is a reality in which we can share. It frees us from the power of the law with its regulations that point us in the right direction, but cannot empower us to live by its precepts. Christ's victory frees us from sin's power which enslaves us to do even the things we don't want to do. And Christ has robbed the evil one of his power. Light and not darkness, freedom and not enslavement, obedience and not rebellion now become a radical possibility for those who put their trust in Christ the victor.

MEDITATION: *In Christ, light and not darkness can become the norm for our lives and for the world.*

Suffering

'The Christian perceives in suffering a temptation of Satan to separate him from God.'

Temptation

Suffering can drive us to the Father's heart to seek his healing care, protection and encouragement. Suffering can also disillusion and embitter us. It can drive us from God with questions born of despair. When the latter occurs, we need to recognise it as a temptation of the evil one. That sort of temptation can only find its mark if we wrongly assume that God's love for us and the reality of suffering don't go together. But they do. We are promised grace, not an absence of difficulty and suffering.

PRAYER: *Father, grant that in my suffering and need I may not lose sight of the One who suffered on my behalf and who also calls me to bear the marks of his suffering in my own body. Amen.*

Cast it off

'Both eye and hand are less than Christ and, when they are used as the instruments of lust and hinder the whole body from the purity of discipleship, they must be sacrificed for the sake of him.'

The Cost of Discipleship

Jesus not only adds a new dimension to our life. He also takes away. What he wishes to take away is anything that hinders our discipleship. And that includes all that is lustful and morally wrong. He calls us to surrender these desires because, eventually, what is born of lust will become hurtful to ourselves and others. Lust desires to possess what it has no right to grasp. This cuts across our discipleship, which calls us not to grasp and to control, but to receive only from God's gracious hand.

THOUGHT: *To lay aside with God's help what may eventually destroy us is not an act of heroism, but one of commonsense.*

September

God maintains the right of life, even
against the man who has grown tired of his life.
He gives man freedom to pledge his life for
something greater, but it is not his will
that man should turn this freedom
arbitrarily against his own life.

Thoughts of suicide

'God maintains the right of life, even against the man who has grown tired of his life. He gives man freedom to pledge his life for something greater, but it is not his will that man should turn this freedom arbitrarily against his own life.'

Ethics

Life is God's gift, but it is our responsibility to make it purposeful. When life lacks meaning, we may be tempted to the point where we despair of life itself. This does not give us the right to take it, but gives us the task only to rediscover its purpose and direction. In this rediscovery, we will need more than care and help; we will need to hear again that life has its centre in the love of God.

THOUGHT: *God has given us the freedom to make choices and to determine our life's direction. But we do not have the freedom to turn against ourselves in negative and destructive ways.*

Not alone

'My burden is borne by the others; their strength is
my strength; when I falter and fail, the faith of the
church comes to my aid.'

Sanctorum Communio

We need to be responsible for our own lives.
But we don't stand alone: the opposite should
be true. We should be deeply embedded in the
life of the Christian community so that when
we falter and fail we can be restored, helped
and encouraged. The Christian is never to be
alone; the Christian's struggle should be supported by the faith, prayers and care of the
Christian community.   And, of course, the
Christian should provide that level of support
to other community members as well.

THOUGHT: *To be supported by the faith, love and
prayers of others acknowledges the reality of 'the
communion of saints' and expresses an important
key in understanding what it means to be the body
of Christ.*

In the service of love and truth

'The truth still remains the greatest service of love which men can show each other in the community of Christ.'

No Rusty Swords

We are to embrace God's truth as normative for our lives. In the light of that truth we are to live, submitting to its call to change our ways, and to fall in step with its direction. Clearly, we all should encourage each other to live in this way. Thus our love and concern for each other should involve the call to love God's truth and to embrace his ways.

THOUGHT: *We should love the other person with unconditional positive regard. But love, while it may cover a multitude of sins, should be a love that also calls the other to live in the light of God's truth.*

On the way

'We are to learn to understand ourselves now as those who have been placed on the way and no longer can do anything other than walk in it.'
Meditating on the Word

When Christ calls us, he invites us not so much to accept a spiritual experience, but to embrace a whole new way of living. As we embrace the beginnings of this journey, we have little idea of what we may encounter further down the road. Blessings come as unexpected surprises, and difficulties come at inappropriate times. And as we journey on, the sheer weight of our ongoing commitment may press in upon us. At times we may be sorely tempted to forsake this journey. But where else can we go? No-one else has the words of eternal life.

THOUGHT: *Our commitment to Christ commits us to a life journey where we are continuously called to follow in Christ's way.*

Come as you are

'You are a sinner, a great, desperate sinner; now come, as the sinner that you are to God who loves you. He wants you as you are; he does not want anything from you, a sacrifice, a work; he wants you alone.'

Life Together

In human affairs, we often gain the impression that people want us or like us because they can get something from us. It is therefore hard for us to understand that God does not first of all ask things from us, but wishes to impart life to us. What is even harder for us to accept is that this God not only welcomes us when we are good, but more particularly when we need his forgiveness.

PRAYER: *Lord, help me that my shame, guilt or fear may never keep me from approaching you with the promise of your grace and forgiveness. Amen.*

A greater power

'Either the Adam in me is tempted — in which case
we fall. Or the Christ in us is tempted — in which
case Satan is bound to fall.'

Temptation

Standing alone without the grace of God is
never a place of safety and security. In fact, it is
the place where we are tempted and seduced.
The place of safety is to live by the promises of
God and the empowering of his Spirit. There
we will also be tempted but need not be
seduced, for Christ the victor will strengthen us
to withstand the enemy.

MEDITATION: *Greater is he that is in us, than he
that is in the world.*

Thank you

'O heavenly Father,
I praise and thank you
For the peace of the night.
I praise and thank you for this new day;
I praise and thank you for all your
goodness and faithfulness throughout
my life.'

Prayer from Prison

W e soon discover that our life is not the result
of our own willing and doing. Its quality of
richness does not lie in a gloating attitude
regarding our own achievements. Instead,
life's rich tapestry is something that we weave
when we appreciate and thank the Giver of life.
This Giver is the God who loves us in Christ,
and who not only protects us, but journeys
with us.

PRAYER: *Father, for your peace and protection I
thank you. I rejoice in your goodness towards me.
But above all, I appreciate your faithfulness and commitment to me as someone who is fickle and far from
consistent. Amen.*

The communion of saints .

'Three great possibilities for acting positively for one
another are disclosed in the communion of saints:
renunciatory, active work for our neighbour; prayers
of intercession; and lastly, the mutual granting of forgiveness of sins in God's name.'

Sanctorum Communio

The beauty of the Christian life does not only lie
in the quality of our relationship with God, but
also in our relationships with one another. Active
helpfulness, intercessory prayer and mutual forgiveness are essential expressions of the kind of
relationships that we should develop. If we only
pray, but do not help, we fall into the trap of
spiritualising things. If we only help, but do not
pray, we run the risk of doing things in our own
strength. And if we do not grant and receive forgiveness, we place ourselves open to idealising
our friends and harbouring hurts in the difficult
journey of serving our sisters and brothers.

MEDITATION: *In prayer I receive, in serving I give,
in being forgiven I am renewed, and in forgiving
others I express the nature of Christ.*

Home

'The homes of men are not, like the shelters of animals, merely the means of protection against bad weather and the night, or merely places for rearing the young; they are places in which a man may relish the joys of his personal life in the intimacy and security of his family and of his property.'

Ethics

We live in houses, but homes need to be created. And we do this when we make room for togetherness, intimacy and sharing and when we create a setting for openness, relaxation and joy. The home should not be like a busy railway station, where we may see each other regularly, but our lives do not really touch. Instead, at our meal times, times for games and story-telling and in the common participation of making the household work, we weave a tradition of togetherness that enriches our lives. This setting also becomes the opportunity for hospitality.

THOUGHT: *If home is no longer the place of intimacy and sharing, where in the world do we then go?*

Forgiveness of sins

'The forgiveness of sins still remains the sole ground of all peace.'

No Rusty Swords

The forgiveness of sins is receiving from God the good news that he will not hold our wrongdoing against us. This is a wonderfully freeing experience, for it is the ground of our peace with God. Receiving forgiveness from those we have wronged and to whom we have gone with our confession and apology is also a liberating experience, for it frees the wrongdoer from guilt and the one who was wronged from anger or bitterness. This also creates peace. In fact, it creates true peace because it flows from reconciliation.

MEDITATION: *True peace is not an uneasy truce; it is the fruit of genuine openness and forgiveness.*

Sharing our thoughts

'But I can't help sharing my thoughts with you, for the simple reason that that's the only way I can clarify my own mind.'

Letters and Papers from Prison

One of the wonderful things about true friendship is that with friends we can speak openly and exploratively. In this setting we do not need to be careful about every word we say. We can speak our mind and 'put it all out in the open'. We can do this because we know that we will be sympathetically listened to. This process will be helpful even if the friend does not give us much feedback. The very fact that we could share our thoughts in this way is itself helpful.

THOUGHT: *True friendship creates the space where one can freely speak one's mind without the fear of being rejected or misunderstood.*

At rest in God?

'All human strivings and drives are finally directed towards God and can only find their complete satisfaction in him.'

Meditating on the Word

Made in God's image, we are moved by the question of ultimate meaning and, in the pursuit of seeking answers, we are faced with questions about God's existence and his involvement in our lives. But we are not likely to receive complete answers to these questions. Moreover, our hearts are not fully at rest when we find our peace with God. We will continue to be troubled by ongoing questions regarding God's involvement and will for our lives. Struggle and the ongoing journey of discipleship are more the order of the day than rest and arrival.

PRAYER: *Father, I thank you for the measure of certainty, protection and peace you have given me. But I also wish to register my ongoing struggles and questions. Help me to live in faith and hope without seeking for final answers, until I meet you face to face. Amen.*

No final solution

'Everywhere the attempt [has been made] to have the kingdom of God present not only to faith but to sight.'   *Sanctorum Communio*

History is replete with Christian attempts to achieve some point of finality. There have been those who have claimed that they know the date of the Lord's return. Others have claimed that they have the right doctrine, the true form of Christian community, or that they constitute a final renewal movement. Behind these claims lies the desire to achieve some point of ultimateness, security and certainty. However noble these desires may be, they finally lead us astray and produce rigidity or idolatry. For the Christian life is not one of certainty, but one of faith; not one of security, but one of risk; not one of ultimateness, but one of hope; and one of journey rather than of safe arrival.

MEDITATION: *The one thing that is certain is that we — with all our ideas, structures and institutions, doctrines and principles — will need to experience ongoing change in the light of God's word and the work of his Spirit.*

Compassion for the suffering

'The thesis that innocent sick life may be properly destroyed in the interest of healthy life. . . springs from the superhuman endeavour to free human society from what appears to be meaningless disease.'

Ethics

Just as we will always have the poor with us, those with disabilities will always be part of the human community. The way in which we are to respond to persons with a disability is not to be one of pity or of isolation, but one of empowerment where they have the opportunity, with support and encouragement, to experience the risks and challenges of life and thereby grow to their full potential.

THOUGHT: *Care must not simply keep people safe, but must encourage them to risk and growth.*

Doubt

'Suddenly doubt has been sowed in his heart; suddenly everything is uncertain.'

Temptation

The Christian does not always live in a state of certainty regarding his faith. The fact that we change and grow in our understanding of God means that previous certainties will need to be replaced by new ones. It is not only change, however, but also unexpected events or disappointments that can shake our certainties and lead to doubt. Doubt itself is not unproductive, for it can be the intermediate step to new certainties.

MEDITATION: *Doubts which are embraced as being the final word are dangerous, while doubts which are seen to be an intermediate step can lead us forward.*

In the middle

'Man no longer lives in the beginning — he has lost the beginning. Now he finds he is in the middle, knowing neither the end nor the beginning.'

Creation and Fall

We cannot go back to a pristine and innocent time where humanity was free and without sin. Nor can we lunge into the future where God's kingdom is fully established and righteousness and peace will reign supreme. Both the beginning and the future are denied us, for we are in the middle. Yet both affect us, for that innocent beginning reminds us that sin and disobedience are not intrinsic to our lives and the future beckons us with the promise of God's new world. This does not make life in the middle undesirable; it only makes it full of promise and tension.

THOUGHT: *The 'not yet' dimension of the Christian life is the seed bed of hope and faith.*

Possessing Christ

'It is only all men together who can possess Christ entirely, and yet each man possesses him entirely too.'

Sanctorum Communio

My personal experience and understanding of Christ is a limited one. I therefore need the faith and understanding of other Christians — and particularly those from other cultures — to enrich my own. We constantly run the danger of making Christ in our own image and of subjecting what Christ tells us to the constraints and concerns of our own culture. In doing this, we run the danger that we only possess the Christ who suits us and serves our ends. If we are to possess Christ more fully or, rather, if he is to possess us, we need to embrace the Christ who is both for us, but who also calls our values into question.

THOUGHT: *No matter how much Christ is for us, he will always challenge our vision, theology and priorities.*

The joys of the body

'It is in the joys of the body that it becomes apparent that the body is an end in itself.'

Ethics

Christianity is not prudish. It celebrates the beauty of creation and rejoices in the way God has made us. It makes room for bodily pleasure, sexuality, comfort and intimacy, but always within a framework of care and responsibility. For the Christian, neither asceticism nor licentiousness are credible options, but only passion and pleasure within the circle of *agape* love that serves the other and does not simply take or demand.

MEDITATION: *If we cannot celebrate the beauty of the way God has made us, we will equate prudishness with spirituality and thus subvert God's generous intention for our lives.*

Christ's honour

'In all that we say and do, we are concerned with
nothing but Christ and his honour among men.'

No Rusty Swords

In proclaiming the relevance of Christ for our
world, we need to make sure that it is Christ's
message that we are sharing and living and not
simply our convenient version of it. If we live
the convenient version, Christ's name will not
be honoured, no matter what we say. If we live
the costly version, his name will be honoured,
though it may not be understood and
embraced by others. The central issue regarding Christ's honour will always be linked to the
way that we represent him in the world.

THOUGHT: *Most people do not have a problem
with Jesus of Nazareth, but they do have difficulty
with the church which claims to represent him on
earth.*

The church at prayer

'The devil fears a roof of thatch beneath which the church is at prayer more than he does a splendid church in which many masses are celebrated.'

Sanctorum Communio

When a church is at prayer much can happen, but this can only take place when the church's prayer has to do with an earnest seeking of God's will. Little happens when the church's prayer is focussed on seeking God's blessing for its own ends. Such prayer is understandable, for we do need God to be our present help in trouble. But transforming prayer occurs when we move from the struggle of our own concerns to the quietude of surrender to God and the activism of a commitment to do what he asks of us.

THOUGHT: *Prayer is the genuine starting point for true activism.*

The many-sidedness of life

'Pain and joy are also part of the polyphony of life,
and. . . they can exist independently side by side.'

Letters and Papers from Prison

The Christian life is not monochrome. It is
varied and diverse. It has answers, but also
questions. There is strength, but also weakness.
It is purposeful, but also uncertain. Pain and
joy, forgiveness and guilt, striving and rest,
peace and conflict, and faith and fear all mingle
together to form the rich texture of life. Thus
the Christian life is never simplistic, but complex. It is never easy, but hard, even though it
can be rich with joy.

PRAYER: *Lord, while we may wish for simple
answers and quick solutions, we thank you that
your grace is with us in the complexity and struggle
of our life of faith. Amen.*

The matter of rights

'One can have a natural right of one's own only if
one respects the natural rights of others.'

Ethics

We all have certain inalienable rights which
are usually enshrined in a nation's legislation.
The centrepiece to these rights is the notion of
freedom and self-determination. But since we
are all part of the human community, the state
and the family, freedom cannot simply mean
freedom for me, but also freedom for others. So
whenever I think of my own rights, I need to
embrace the responsibility of thinking about
the rights of others as well.

THOUGHT: *Rights are as much a responsibility as
they are a privilege.*

Flee

'There is no resistance to Satan other than flight. . .
Flee — that can indeed only mean flee to that place
where you find protection and help, flee to the
Crucified.'

Temptation

All of us are vulnerable to certain kinds of
temptation. For some it may be greed, for
others power and for others lust. We are usually well aware of our particular weaknesses.
One constructive form of action is to stay away
from what readily tempts us, but this may force
many to virtually withdraw from life. Therefore, a more constructive action is not just to
flee, but to flee to Christ for his purging and
empowering.

PRAYER: *Lord, I come to you acknowledging my
weakness and vulnerability. I pray not only for
your protection, but more particularly for your
strengthening and transformation. Amen.*

The cycle of each day

'In the morning the unformed becomes form and by evening sinks back into formlessness. The bright polarity of light dissolves into unity with the darkness. Living sound grows silent in the stillness of the night.'

Creation and Fall

Life has its rhythm of day and night, spring and summer, and birth and death. There is also a time to be still and a time to act. In the cycle of each new day hurrying to meet evening's dark caress, we have a reminder, not only of the reality of time and the limited nature of our own life, but also of the joy of new beginnings. More particularly, the genius of the Old Testament concept of time is that it begins with evening and with rest and issues into the activity of the next day.

THOUGHT: *God worked and then rested. His gift to us is that we rest first and then embrace the activity of each new day.*

The framework of life

'Thus for the sake of Christ and his coming, natural life must be lived within the framework of certain definite rights and certain definite duties.'

Ethics

The Christian's concern should never only be for the church and for God's kingdom, but also for natural life and the world. Our concerns should include good government, equal opportunity, justice, values that ennoble the human person, as well as concerns for our environment and the world's resources. These concerns are not secular. Rather they are deeply spiritual, for without a sustainable world and cultural values based on freedom and justice, the message of God's love revealed in Jesus Christ would fall into a vacuum.

THOUGHT: *The God of the Bible is Creator as well as Redeemer. He is concerned about life as much as he is concerned about eternal life.*

God at the edge

'God is being increasingly edged out of the world now that it has come of age. Knowledge and life are thought to be perfectly possible without him.'
Letters and Papers from Prison

We are living in a world which is bursting with discoveries and new knowledge. In such a world, the significance of God appears to be shrinking in the wake of the awesome progress of science. Christians are therefore tempted to make their faith more and more esoteric, other-worldly. Yet precisely the opposite should be taking place; our faith should be made relevant to this new knowledge. For while science may answer many of the 'what' questions, Christian faith can be directed to the 'why' questions that have to do with purpose, meaning and application.

THOUGHT: *The progress of knowledge can never edge out the reality of faith in a God who has revealed himself in Jesus Christ. It can only edge out a God whom we have tied too closely to our limited understanding of life and the universe.*

The rule of love

'God's will to rule is his will to love his church.'
Sanctorum Communio

An approach that gives when it has the right to demand is a remarkable quality of love indeed. An attitude that forgives when it could condemn and a love that embraces us when it could so easily find reason to reject us is a love that inspires hope and faith. God's love does the opposite to what we would normally expect. It fills empty rather than full hands. It pursues the worst to make it the best. It makes the weak strong and rules with love rather than with force or coercion.

MEDITATION: *If only we could be satisfied with rejoicing in the love that God has for us, we would be far richer than if we had all the blessings that we so ardently seek.*

Christ in the face of my neighbour

'Christians always see other men as brethren to whom Christ comes; they meet them only by going to them with Jesus.'

The Cost of Discipleship

Everyone that we meet, be they neighbour or stranger, is a person made in God's image and is therefore a person of worth and dignity. Yet, like ourselves, that person also bears the marks of the fall and of sin, and is therefore a candidate for the restorative love of God in Christ. While we should reach out to others in friendship and interest simply for their own sake and not only in order to evangelise them, we do need to meet them with Christ in our hearts and in the hope that they, too, will meet him who is the giver of life.

THOUGHT: *The Christ in our hearts is the good shepherd who seeks that which is lost. We cannot but walk with him unless we walk in the footsteps of his concern.*

Those inner desires

'When you have deliberately suppressed every desire for so long, it burns you up inside, or else you get so bottled up that one day there is a terrific explosion.'

Letters and Papers from Prison

We all have desires for love, sexuality, success, appreciation and significance. All our desires are not always fulfilled, just as all our needs are not always met. This can be due to our particular circumstances at a given time. It can also be due to the choices that we have made. What is important, however, is that we face our unfulfilled desires and needs and seek God's answers to our dilemmas. Those answers may not always provide a way of escape, a solution or a sublimation. They may simply be a surrender to the impenetrability of God's purpose for us.

MEDITATION: *Facing that which is unfulfilled in our lives is learning to face an abyss over which there are a few rope bridges.*

Full or empty

'Prayer does not mean simply to pour out one's
heart. It means rather to find the way to God and to
speak with him, whether the heart is full or empty.'

Psalms: The Prayer Book of the Bible

Prayer is not only appropriate when we have
much to say to God either in thanksgiving or
with our requests. Prayer is also appropriate
when we have nothing to say, when our thanks
languishes in our hearts and our requests have
become numb through disappointment or
delay. When we are in such circumstances, our
prayers will not be elegant, but they can be
powerful, for they come as a heart-cry to the
God who alone can bring hope and salvation.

PRAYER: *Father, grant that when my heart is
empty and hope and faith have failed me, that I will
still bring my heart-cry to you. Amen.*

October

*Christianity plunges us
into many different
dimensions of life
simultaneously...
we weep with those
who weep, and rejoice
with those who rejoice.*

Multi-dimensional

'Christianity plunges us into many different dimensions of life simultaneously. We can make room in
our hearts, to some extent at least, for God and the
whole world. We weep with those that weep, and
rejoice with those that rejoice.'

Letters and Papers from Prison

The Christian is always to resist the temptation
to become one-sided and to reduce complexity
to simple solutions. It is never easy to bring
together in one's own experience a love for God
and a spirituality that stresses holiness, and an
engagement with the world that involves us in
caring and long-term action. Yet this is precisely the challenge, for in Christ, whom we are to
follow, we see the meeting of God and man,
heaven and earth, power and weakness.

THOUGHT: *Just as a husband or wife love each
other and their children differently, so we can love
both God and our world.*

God's creation

'He [God] is bound not to the work, but he binds
the work to himself.'

Creation and Fall

God is not limited to his creation. He preceded
it and is greater than the things he called into
being. But the creation cannot exist without
God's maintenance and care. Similarly, we
should not limit ourselves to the things we do.
We also are more than the work of our hands,
although we, too, may need to maintain the
things we have made and done, lest they fall
into chaos or disrepair.

THOUGHT: *Our work faces the threat of chaos and
disintegration and therefore needs to be maintained,
although in the final analysis we cannot fully maintain what we have made or done. We thus need to
commit our work to God's keeping and care.*

God's work of preservation

'The natural is the form of life preserved by God for the fallen world and directed towards justification, redemption and renewal through Christ.'

Ethics

God is at work in our world not only through the instrumentality of the church, but also through the reality of work, family, government and through those who work for justice, mercy and peace. This is not to say that *all* work and government reflect God's intention, but only that which conforms to his revealed will. Therefore, while we should rejoice in God's common gift of a sustainable world, marriage, labour and the good order of society, we should remember that God's desire is that all these should reflect the redemptive work of his Son.

MEDITATION: *Christians should not only work redemptively in the world, but should also work to preserve that which promotes the common good.*

Temptation to forgetfulness

'Satan does not here fill us with hatred of God, but with forgetfulness of God.'

Temptation

The greatest form of punishment that can be handed out to another human being is not acts of aggression, but to be ignored and to be subject to the slow, painful effect of neglect. This destroys the other. It makes the other a non-person. Similarly, the greatest temptation is not to be angry with God, but to gradually ignore him to the point where he is no longer relevant for those things that are important features of our lives.

PRAYER: *Father, grant that when my relationship with you becomes problematical, may I continue to actively engage you in an attempt at resolution and not simply begin to ignore you. Amen.*

Praying in the right way

'If we are to pray aright, perhaps it is quite necessary that we pray contrary to our own heart.'
Psalms: The Prayer Book of the Bible

Prayer is speaking and listening. Not only do we need to speak to God and listen to what he may say to us, but we also need to listen more carefully to what our own hearts are saying. Sometimes what is in our hearts is inconsistent with what is on our lips and sometimes what is in our hearts is far removed from that which only seeks God's honour and his kingdom. We therefore need to pray that our motivations, desires and intentions will be purified by the light of God's word and the purging of his Spirit.

THOUGHT: *Our motivations, desires and intentions can be complex and are often not single-minded. Moreover, there is much that we do from mixed motives. This needs to be faced honestly if we are to continue with some sense of integrity.*

Love for our neighbour

'My communion of love with my neighbour can subsist only in faith in God.'

Sanctorum Communio

My neighbour is that special person whom circumstances place within my sphere of contact. Not everyone is neighbour to my neighbour, but I and a small group of others are. This brings with it special opportunities and blessings, for in my neighbour I can experience something of God's general design for human community. I can also experience something of the reciprocity that makes life rich. And by faith I can see my neighbour as the one for whom Christ died.

MEDITATION: *In the face of my neighbour I can see the hope for human community, mutual respect, mutual care and the potentiality for a mutual celebration of the love and goodness of God.*

God's presence in our world

'Lord Jesus, when I am tempted because I cannot see God and his power and love in this world, let me firmly look upon you, for you are my Lord and my God.'

Meditating on the Word

We will probably never see enough of God's presence and action in our world, for his action is hidden as much as it is open to view. He is there when we don't expect him and he is ahead of us, calling us into his will and direction for our lives. It is therefore by faith that we live, experiencing touches of his presence, touching the edges of his ways, embracing his promises, and longing for the day when our faith will eventually be sight.

THOUGHT: *Even when we see God's action in our world, we will only see that with the eyes of faith.*

The church and the message of God

'The church must be able to say the word of God, the word of authority, here and now, in the most concrete way possible, from knowledge of the situation.'

No Rusty Swords

What the church says is not only a message for the people of God, but also for the world. That word must be more than merely a word that rails against the moral evils of society. It must be a word that champions freedom, promotes responsibility, encourages justice, inspires hope, makes room for mercy and calls for accountability.

THOUGHT: *The church is often good at telling the rest of the world what it should not do. But its vision for a positive direction is often missing.*

Dealing with our guilt

'Indeed, the tempter is only to be found where there
is innocence; for where there is guilt, he has already
gained power.'

Temptation

Innocence is never the place of safety, for that is
where we can be tempted. But guilt need never
be the place of despair, for our wrongdoing can
be confessed and forgiven. Guilt that is unac-
knowledged and undealt-with becomes the
place of danger, for guilt will always cause us
to react in unhelpful and sometimes destructive
ways. Moreover, undealt-with guilt often
makes us blame others or causes us to compen-
sate in ways that camouflage the real issues.
The tempter's power in our guilt can be broken,
but he will always attempt to catch us from behind when we think that all is safe and well.

PRAYER: *Father, grant that when all appears to be
well, I may be on my guard. And that when I am
trapped by guilt, I may run to you with my confession. Amen.*

God's commands

'It is grace to know God's commands. They release us from self-made plans and conflicts.'

Psalms: The Prayer Book of the Bible

God's commandments provide us with a framework for our lives. From them we learn, among other things, that life is precious, that it cannot be violated and that we cannot take from our neighbour what is not ours. But it is our responsibility to paint the details of the picture within this framework. It is one thing to know that we cannot take from our neighbour what is not ours, but another to know how to affirm and to be as Christ to that neighbour. For the final intention of the law is not to set boundaries for what we *should not* do, but to motivate us to love God and our neighbour in the same way as we love ourselves.

MEDITATION: *God's law provides the framework for a life of responsibility and love.*

Sustained by the world

'I belong to this world completely. It bears me, nourishes me and holds me.'

Creation and Fall

It is not only God who sustains life, but it is also the world which he has made which nourishes and supports me. God's goodness to me is not always directly displayed. Much of God's nurture and care comes indirectly. It comes through the good earth he has made, the social institutions that reflect the reality of human freedom and care, and it comes through the love, support and encouragement of others. For this reason, Christians should not only be concerned with proclaiming and promoting God's direct action of grace and mercy, but also be actively involved in caring for our world and the institutions of our land.

THOUGHT: *We are called to promote all that which sustains and enhances life and not only that which promotes eternal life.*

Listening to scripture

'[It is pointless] to go about the interpretation in such a way that the biblical message is passed through the sieve of man's own knowledge — what will not go through is scorned and tossed away.'

No Rusty Swords

Clearly we never come to the Bible with a blank slate, but with the issues and concerns of our time. These issues help form the questions that we wish to ask of scripture. This is appropriate, providing that we then listen carefully to what scripture has to say, even to the point of allowing it to modify our concerns and anticipated answers. What should not be acceptable is that we prejudge scripture by our own knowledge and values. This stills the voice of the Bible. It means that we only accept what fits in with us. Thus we use the Bible as a mirror which reflects back to us what we already know, rather than seeing it as a conversation partner that reflects a wisdom that is worth listening to.

THOUGHT: *The Bible is clearly a book that was written in a past age. But throughout its pages there pulsates a wisdom that we can hear anew as God speaking.*

Love for God and the world

'God requires that we should love him eternally with our whole hearts, yet not so as to compromise or diminish our earthly affections.'

Letters and Papers from Prison

Love for God and love for the world are not opposed to each other. Rather the opposite is true, namely, that love for God deepens our love for the world. Many Christians have the idea that true love for God should diminish our concern for the world, and that concern for the world will diminish our love for God. The latter is always a risk that we boldly need to take, because the former is a serious distortion of the lesson of Jesus.

THOUGHT: *There is no greater illustration of the fact that God is opposed to asceticism than in the incarnation.*

Self and service

'The desire for one's own honour hinders faith. One who seeks for his own honour is no longer seeking God and his neighbour.'

Life Together

We need to be our own person. We cannot embrace the love of God and the service to our neighbour in such a way that we leave ourselves behind. Service is not self-negation, but it is the voluntary bringing of ourselves to a particular situation of need. But service does cut across our own priorities and, more specifically, should cut across the selfishness of the self where even in the serving of others, it still seeks to serve only the self.

MEDITATION: *The self needs to be nurtured and sustained. If this is to occur in a wholesome manner, then the self must also serve the other. But the true service of the other is not to feed the self, but to empower the other.*

The power of desire

'With irresistible power, desire seizes mastery over the flesh. . . it makes no difference whether it is sexual desire, or ambition, or vanity, or desire for revenge, or love of fame and power, or greed for money.'

Temptation

Desire is a strong unfulfilled longing that drives us to attain what we believe we need or should have. As such, it is a potentially creative force. It can move us out of the unsatisfactory nature of the present into the hope of a more fulfilled future. But desire can also become a dominating power that drives us to achieve at any cost. It can move us to grasp for that which should be undesirable: revenge, greed and fame. Human desire, therefore, must always operate within the framework of God's will.

THOUGHT: *To desire to do God's will is the greatest way we can be creatively motivated, for God's will is never law, but the way of freedom he holds before us.*

He knows our suffering

'Lord Jesus Christ, you were poor and in distress, a captive and forsaken as I am. You know all man's troubles.'

Prayer from Prison

To know that others experience similar difficulties and struggles to the ones we are going through is usually of little comfort and help. This does not lessen our pain or distress. But when others come to weep with us, bring comfort and practical help, the burden is lessened. Christ is not meant to be a distant reminder to us that he also suffered, but is the One who enters into our present distress and loneliness, to encourage and empower us even though he may not always bring deliverance and escape.

MEDITATION: *Jesus is not only the suffering man of Golgotha, but also the present Lord who lives with us through the Holy Spirit.*

Alone

'The first man is alone. Christ was also alone. And we are alone as well.'

Creation and Fall

The rhythm of life is one of withdrawal and participation, one of being alone and being a part of community, and one of closedness and openness. The triad of withdrawal, being alone and closedness should never be weighted negatively against that of participation, community and openness. Withdrawal is necessary if we are to retain the energy for active participation. Closedness is necessary to guard the sacredness of our own person so that in an engaging openness we do not lose ourselves. And finally, loneliness is as intrinsic to our being as is community. In being alone we not only affirm the individuality of the 'I', but we also experience the possibility of dread which can only move us to thankfulness for the gift of fellowship and friendship.

MEDITATION: *To be alone is not to be lost. It is a way of finding ourselves in the midst of the human community.*

Fear of the concrete command

'If Jesus challenged us with the command: "Get out of it", we [are likely to] take him to mean: "Stay where you are, but cultivate that inward detachment".'

The Cost of Discipleship

We love to spiritualise things, and we are good at reducing the specific to vague generalisations. We are equally good at making the disturbing words of scripture seem reasonable and making the concrete command a nebulous attitude. Thus the command to forsake something easily becomes the vague attitude of inner detachment to the things we are meant to leave behind. In taking this approach we will never offend anyone, but we will never change anyone either — least of all ourselves.

MEDITATION: *If we are happy to embrace the blessings and promises of Jesus, we can do no less than also to embrace his words of correction and direction.*

Either/or

'Radicalism hates time, and compromise hates eternity. Radicalism hates patience, and compromise hates decision. Radicalism hates wisdom, and compromise hates simplicity.'

Ethics

Every motivation, no matter how good, needs to be counter-balanced lest it becomes distorted. Love for another needs to be balanced by the freedom of the other, lest love becomes possessive and stifling. Every system and program, no matter how right it may initially seem, will need to be modified, for its very strength and virtue will finally become its undoing. Neither radicalism nor compromise, dominance nor submission, independence nor dependence are equally good options, for neither work in the long run. We are therefore faced with the difficult task of finding some middle way. This middle way is not the act of compromise, but the way of true wisdom.

THOUGHT: *Neither rugged individualism nor rigid communitarianism should characterise our lives as Christians, but a mutuality which calls us to freedom and responsibility.*

Prayers for vengeance

'The prayer for the vengeance of God is the prayer
for the execution of his righteousness in the judgment of sin.'

Psalms: The Prayer Book of the Bible

As Christians we can pray the prayers of the
Psalms, including the prayers for vengeance.
Such prayers have nothing to do with personal
retaliation. We are not to curse our enemies,
but to bless them. But we are to pray that
God's righteousness and justice will be
manifest in our world. This means that we are
asking that proud oppressors will be humbled
and that the poor and needy will be lifted up
out of the ash-heap of their lives.

MEDITATION: *The prayer for the vengeance of God
can only come from one whose concern is to see
God's righteousness manifest in our world.*

Satan in pursuit

'Because Satan could not bring about the fall of the
Son of God, he pursues him now with all temptations in his members.'

Temptation

Satan does not always pursue Christians, for
Christians do not always pose a threat. There
are times when Christians are compromised,
guilt-ridden and ineffectual. At such times the
Accuser does not need to pursue them, for they
are already within the ambit of his influence.
But when the Christian is at prayer, is seeking
to do God's will, confesses guilt and wrongdoing, obeys the impulses of the Spirit and pursues justice and mercy, then the Evil One will
be in pursuit seeking to disrupt and to destroy.

THOUGHT: *Satan is never the final threat. The
greater threat is our own disobedience.*

God as stop-gap

'It has been brought home to me how wrong it is to use God as a stop-gap for the incompleteness of our knowledge.'

Letters and Papers from Prison

If God is simply seen as a means of explaining what science has not yet been able to explain, then not only may we eventually crowd God out of our world, but we are relegating him to only a part of life. And more seriously, we are defining him as irrelevant for our technological world. The opposite should be the case. The more our knowledge of the world grows, the more we should be celebrating God's wisdom in creating this world, and the more we should be grappling with how God's revelation in scripture guides our understanding of what kind of world we ought to have that technology is shaping.

THOUGHT: *The more our world is technologically shaped, the more pressing becomes the question of the meaning, purpose, direction and quality of such a world. For this, God's revelation in scripture has an answer.*

God's Spirit and the Bible

'God's Spirit battles only through the word of scripture and of confession.'

No Rusty Swords

Spiritual enthusiasts always come with the claim that the Spirit personally told them to do this or that. That may well be the case, but God's Spirit does not work apart from the Bible and the Bible cannot be understood apart from the Spirit's guidance. Thus the Spirit's direction is not something that is privately mysterious, but is something that should be publicly open. This does not mean that the Spirit may not reveal something new. But usually the new is something old in scripture that has been neglected.

MEDITATION: *There is much in God's word that we neglect or ignore. This the Spirit seeks to bring to our attention, if we are searching for truth.*

The fruit of our labour is a gift

'Thus the fruits of the field become both the bread which we eat with tears and the bread of charity of him who sustains us.'

Creation and Fall

Life in the world is refractory and our work is marked by difficulty. The good which we seek to do bears its fruit, but also has, at times, unintended and negative consequences. Yet from our labour we do reap some reward. This must never be regarded as our right, but must be seen as a gift from God who providentially cares for us.

THOUGHT: *In our daily labour there are some things which we have to wrestle into being, while at other times that which we thought would be almost impossible just falls into place. For the latter, we can only thank God for his gift of creativity, and for the former the blessing of perseverance.*

When to stop

'Don't try and do too much.'

Letters and Papers from Prison

Some people are lazy and constantly need to be encouraged and motivated. Others are very intense and active and need to be encouraged to disengage and learn to be still lest they over-tax their finite resources. While laziness is the failure to face responsibility in life, driven activity is the failure to appreciate God's grace and our personal limitation.

MEDITATION: *Doing much is never in itself a virtue. It only is a virtue when the much is placed at the behest of the other and not in the cause of self-aggrandisement.*

The new humanity

'The church. . . is a communion created by Christ and founded upon him, one in which Christ reveals himself as. . . the new humanity itself.'

Act and Being

The basic purpose of Christ's coming into the world easily becomes obscured. It is often said that Christ has only come to give eternal life and the forgiveness of our sins. This obscures the more fundamental purpose of his coming: namely, that he is the head of the new humanity which is called to pattern its life in discipleship on that of Christ.

THOUGHT: *If we wish to embrace Christ's salvation and forgiveness, we must grasp his call to be his followers in faith and commitment.*

The heart-cry of the Psalms

'Serious illness and severe loneliness before God and men, threat, persecution, imprisonment and whatever conceivable peril there is on earth are known by the Psalms.'

Psalms: The Prayer Book of the Bible

The Psalms express the full spectrum of the human condition, including joy and despair, faith and doubt, exultation and despondency, and peace and turmoil. In the Psalms we can recognise ourselves, but we can also hear the writer's struggle of faith. This should encourage us in our own spiritual journey, for the Psalms do not provide easy answers and do not suggest that the walk of faith is smooth and simple.

THOUGHT: *To know that others have walked a similar road may not make the difficulties of the journey easier, but should give us hope.*

Divided

'The healthy man is borne up in pain and nourished by that which is full of pleasure; he is torn in pleasure by pain, in good he is torn by evil, in evil he is torn by good. He is divided.'

Creation and Fall

In pain, we can experience comfort and in distress, hope. In difficulty, we can experience practical help and in our loneliness, friendship. But in our comfort, we can also experience sadness and in our hope, an element of despair. In being helped, we can feel vulnerable and in friendship, we can feel trapped. While we may wish that things were not so, they cannot be different. For if they were, we would no longer partake of the human condition.

MEDITATION: *While we are divided between good and evil and hope and despair, Christ's work in our lives seeks to overcome evil and despair.*

The word of the community

'The word of this community is preaching and sacrament; its conduct is believing and loving.'

Act and Being

The Christian church is to be concerned with many things, but its primary task is to build up the faith of its members. It cannot do this only through its ministry of worship and teaching. It also needs to do this through encouraging a life together of its members. Teaching needs to be practically expressed in common encouragement and help. And a common life together of commitment and care will always enrich our understanding of the scriptures.

THOUGHT: *Teaching and conduct, faith and praxis, believing and doing belong together.*

Abandoned

'The Spirit leads Jesus into the wilderness, into solitude, into abandonment. God takes from his Son all help of man and creature.'

Temptation

It is nonsense to say that we will never experience the same abandonment and temptation that Jesus did. Precisely the opposite is the case. But such experiences will only be true of those who seek, in true discipleship, to follow Jesus Christ. Those who live for themselves and seek to protect themselves from the risk of faith and the walk of obedience will not know such experiences. In this they assume that they are in a safe place, yet are in fact lost.

THOUGHT: *To be abandoned and tempted is a safer place to be than to be in the place of safety, which is not characterised by faith and obedience.*

The big issues of life

'Grateful as we are for every bit of private happiness that comes our way, we must not for a moment lose sight of the great causes we are living for, and they must cast light rather than gloom upon your joy.'

Letters and Papers from Prison

The big issues of life can never be our own well-being and security. For in living for Christ, we also live for the concerns and issues of our day. This does not mean that the world sets our agenda, but it does mean that the pressing issues of our time need a Christian response. These issues are usually so big and seemingly insoluble that we can be overwhelmed and lose all sense of perspective. To overcome this, we need to rejoice in what we have, be thankful for any small progress and, more importantly, celebrate the hope that is ours in the knowledge that God has a passion for justice.

MEDITATION: *The great causes are often the small causes that no-one thinks are pressing enough to require immediate action.*

November

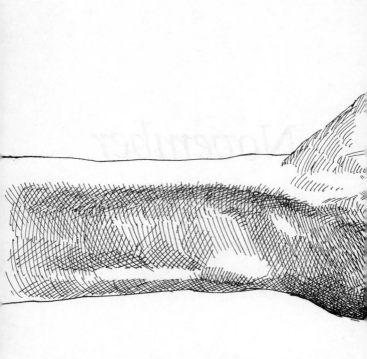

In a Christian community everything
depends upon whether each individual
is an indispensable link in a chain.

Links in a chain

'In a Christian community, everything depends upon whether each individual is an indispensable link in a chain.'

Life Together

The church as an institution continues its life on the basis of its traditions and structures. Where the church functions as a community — based on mutual care and responsibility — its life is sustained through mutual relationships, with each member playing a part. There is a great dynamism, as well as a great vulnerability, in being church in this way. That is why we tend to opt for the church as institution rather than that of community. The value of church as community is that because each person must play a part, each person can also grow in the use of their particular gifts, talents and qualities.

THOUGHT: *Community develops, not from a love of community, but from the love we have for each other.*

Good out of evil

'The Christian. . . remains earthbound, even when his desire is towards God; he must go through all the anxiety before the laws of the world; he must learn the paradox that the world offers us a choice not between good and evil, but between one evil and another, and that nevertheless God leads him to himself even through evil.'

No Rusty Swords

If good always springs from good, then God's redemptive work is not necessary. The miracle of God's grace, however, is that good can be brought forth out of evil, and that even our good needs to be surrendered to the purposes of God and be transformed by his grace.

MEDITATION: *Our good will never be such that it will not need God's participation, and our wrong-doing should always be brought to be transformed by his grace.*

Joy and sorrow

'Joy is rich in fears; sorrow has its sweetness.'

Prayer from Prison

A wonderful experience is never perfect or complete, and a sad or difficult experience is never without some value. For the difficult experiences we need to find the grace of God, and for the joyful experiences we need to express true thankfulness. Difficulties thus need to be transformed and wonderful experiences need to be celebrated.

PRAYER: *Lord, in the varied experiences of life help me to take the good things with simplicity and the difficult things with fortitude. Amen.*

The hope of the future

'It is only out of the future that the present can be lived.'

Act and Being

We need to live the present with all its joys and difficulties, but the future should always beckon us. The future is not significant because we idealistically hope that things may get better, for they may in fact get worse. Rather, the future should beckon us because the God who possesses the future will be ahead of us with new grace, opportunities and hope.

MEDITATION: *If we lose the future — that is, lose our faith and hope in the God who is ahead of us — we will also lose the present.*

The ordinary

'It is precisely in the commonplace surroundings of the everyday that the church is believed and experienced. It is not in the moments of spiritual exaltation, but in the monotony and severity of daily life and in the regular worship of God that we come to understand the church's full significance.'

Sanctorum Communio

Sometimes our life together as church is marked by exaltation and joy. More commonly, it is marked by perseverance and repetition. However, the commonality and ordinary nature of our experience should never be despised. The ordinary is as much a gift of God's grace as the special and extraordinary.

MEDITATION: *The ordinary, all the more, needs the eyes of faith to see its value.*

In flight

'Man has suddenly fallen from God and is still in flight.'

Creation and Fall

We are still in flight. We withhold information. We mask our true feelings. We twist facts. We modify the things we should say. In this and many other ways we demonstrate that openness, truth, transparency and simplicity don't come naturally, but need to be striven for. Innocence is no longer an essential part of who we are. We therefore need constantly to be called to the light, called to accountability and called to the truth.

THOUGHT: *In our flight we hope to free ourselves, but instead we entangle ourselves ever more deeply.*

When all is well

'We must not wait until we are at the end of our tether. [God] must be found at the centre of life: in life, and not only in death; in health and vigour, and not only in suffering; in activity, and not only in sin.'

Letters and Papers from Prison

Living in grateful dependence on God, when we are well and active and in possession of all the things we need for daily life, is a miracle of the grace of God. We need to be kept by the love of God in a far greater measure when all is well than when we are sick or in distress and difficulty.

MEDITATION: *God is not only the Saviour; he is also the providential sustainer of our whole life.*

Change is possible

'The world lives and has its future by means of the blessing of God and of the righteous person.'

Meditating on the Word

No matter how dark and troubled our world may be, God providentially sustains our world and this provides us with the opportunity to work for its betterment. This betterment is always a possibility if we ourselves are changed into the likeness of Christ and delivered from our inherent selfishness.

THOUGHT: *A different world is possible when men and women, who dare to be different, relinquish the royal road of power and embrace the walk of servanthood.*

The good life

'Many earnest Christians are struck as they pray the Psalms by how often the petition for life and good fortune occurs.'

Psalms: The Prayer Book of the Bible

The Psalms speak of many things: the worship of God, deliverance from our enemies, the celebration of God's faithfulness, the struggle of faith and the importance of prayer. The Psalms also recognise that our very life needs to be sustained by God and that well-being, blessing and good fortune come from God's hand and are never simply the result of our own achievements. The Psalms thus recognise that the good that comes our way can be enjoyed, but they also express God's care for the poor. And this fact clearly calls us to responsibility regarding the things that we receive and use.

THOUGHT: *One of our biggest challenges is to replace our ideas of ownership with the idea of stewardship.*

Freedom with others

'Freedom is not something man has for himself, but something he has for others.'

Creation and Fall

Freedom is not a possession we have in and of ourselves. Freedom emerges in relationships and in response to particular situations. Freedom is thus never a static reality; it is something that needs to be gained again and again. Christ does not set us free once. We need to appropriate that freedom again and again, because we are so adept at replacing freedom with form, and grace with law. Freedom, moreover, is only there when it is experienced in concert with others.

THOUGHT: *Freedom is not a personal possession, but a communal reality.*

Reward

'The reward of the righteous is not the happiness or the power or the honour of this world. It is nothing other than the fellowship of the cross of Christ.'

Meditating on the Word

Many Christians quietly and faithfully carry on a variety of ministries that never receive public recognition. The few that do receive such recognition need to draw even more deeply on the life of Christ. For Christ needs to save them from human adulation, pride and furthering their own cause, rather than the cause of the suffering Servant.

THOUGHT: *Human rewards for spiritual service remain an ever-present threat in subverting such service.*

In the church

'To be in Christ. . . means to be in the church.'

The Cost of Discipleship

Most people have no difficulty in acknowledging Christ as an exemplary figure, and many readily acknowledge him as God's Son and Saviour of the world. The church, however, has no such exemplary status and its track record is less than wonderful. So while many people have no problem with Christ, they do have difficulty with the church. Yet to belong to Christ means that we do not remain solitary, but join with others to form the Christian community. The fact that this will always be a less than perfect institution means that, while we should be part of the church, our redemption does not lie there, but in Christ alone.

PRAYER: *Lord, help me to join the church, not as a critic or as a demander, but as one who serves. And more importantly, help me to acknowledge that problems in the church are also my problem. Amen.*

Intercession

'The very time we give to intercession will turn out to be a daily source of new joy in God and in the Christian community.'

Life Together

Prayer for others, rather than for ourselves, is a strangely enriching experience. It not only teaches us to look beyond ourselves and to seek God's face for the welfare of the other, but it makes us see the other in a very different light. The person for whom we pray becomes a person of new possibilities, for our prayer envisages change, renewal, healing and transformation for such a person.

THOUGHT: *Intercessory prayer is a great but secret service that we can offer to others.*

To act

'Forgive my lack of faith and any wrong that I have done today, and help me to forgive all who have wronged me.'

Prayer from Prison

The area where we fail most significantly is not in our actual wrongdoing, but in those areas where we fail to grasp the nettle, fail to take hold of the opportunity, fail to act decisively when we know we must, fail to take the next step that will lead us on a new journey, and fail to take the risk and thus to venture into new territory. Our sin is that we prefer safety to risk and security to the walk of faith. For this we need not only God's forgiveness, but also new courage to try again.

MEDITATION: *Wrongdoing can be forgiven and corrected, but failing to act at all, while seemingly harmless, is more pernicious in its final outworking.*

God's law as demand

'The man who is faced by God's commandment as demand is thrown back upon himself and must live in this way.'

Creation and Fall

There is nothing helpful about God's law as demand, for the law only accentuates our own inability to live according to its precepts. But the law can drive us to Christ and, once having found his grace, can provide us with guidelines for ordering our lives. In the grace of God, we find the true centre for our very being and, in obeying the law, we commit ourselves to constructive ways of living and acting in our world.

PRAYER: *Lord, we thank you for your grace which revolutionises our inner being and sustains us in doing your will. Amen.*

Christ on the road with us

'Only the man who follows the command of Jesus single-mindedly and unresistingly lets his yoke rest upon him, finds his burden easy and, under its gentle pressure, receives the power to persevere in the right way.'

The Cost of Discipleship

Without the word of Jesus for our lives, we may be busy and active, but we cannot be ultimately productive. Nor are we purposefully sustained and encouraged. But in ordering our lives on the word of Jesus, we may find ourselves walking a difficult road. However, on that road we will be kept, for the Master himself is with us.

THOUGHT: *The alternatives are not 'life without the word of Jesus will be easy' and 'life obeying Christ is hard'. Rather the options are 'without the word of Christ, we walk alone' and 'in obeying him, he is with us'.*

Kept

'The Christian knows hours of temptation, which differ from hours of gracious care and preservation from temptation.'

Temptation

The more that we are kept safe and secure, the more that we become candidates for temptation. This is not to suggest that being protected is not a wonderful thing. But we quickly fail to appreciate God's protecting hand over our lives and begin to take things for granted. In this way we become candidates for temptation.

THOUGHT: *The place of safety can only be where we walk humbly with our God, are aware of our vulnerability, and constantly look to him to keep and sustain us.*

Beauty for ashes

'In a flower garden [certain Christians] grub around
for the dung on which the flowers grow.'
Letters and Papers from Prison

Life is made up of problems and difficulties,
but it also has its beauty. Some people only always see the difficulties. Other people have an
unhealthy focus on what is messy, suspicious
and grubby. Both never see the flowers. Yet
conversely, some only ever see the flowers and
fail to see what makes flowers grow. They live
in the world of make-belief. They refuse to face
difficulties and elevate their idealisation above
that of focussing on real people and real situations. Clearly, this is no way to live either.
Beauty needs to be born out of real life, which
includes our weaknesses and difficulties.

THOUGHT: *Out of the ash-heap of our lives, God
brings forth his beauty.*

The strong and the weak

'The weak must not judge the strong; the strong must not despise the weak.'

Life Together

Every church has those who are mature and strong, and those who are immature and weak. But such distinctions are never accurate. The weak have their particular gifts to bring and contributions to make, while the strong have weaknesses with which they need to deal. The strong need to encourage the weak without making them dependent, while the weak need to follow the example of the strong without putting them on a pedestal.

THOUGHT: *The final criteria is never whether one is strong or weak, but whether one is growing, learning, giving and receiving.*

One church

'We should really be *one* church.'

No Rusty Swords

The disunity of the Christian church is a sore that runs through much of the church's two-thousand-year history. On the other hand, the richness of the biblical writings is such that their truth could hardly be contained within a single organisational structure.   While organisational unity may not be achievable or even desirable, Christians are nevertheless one in Christ and should express that fact in practical cooperation.

MEDITATION: *If unity is not organic, practical and grassroots, it may not be worth having.*

Being justified

'Only man can be justified, precisely because only
[Jesus] who is justified becomes "man".'

Ethics

We are moved at the very centre of our existence by the question of God. Not only in nature but also in the long tradition of our
Western culture the question of God's existence
presses itself upon us. This question never sits
easily with us for we are both attracted by God
and afraid of him. We have doubt as well as
faith. This struggle will never be finally settled
until we embrace God's love revealed in Jesus
Christ. In this embrace we need not be overwhelmed, for in Christ we become more truly
ourselves. For Christ as the second Adam mir-
rors for us the kind of person we are becoming.
In him we find our true being as we live by his
words, grace and Spirit.

THOUGHT: *Being justified means that we have
come home, having been welcomed by the Father
who ever beckons us.*

Power of God's word

'He who can speak out of the abundance of God's word, the wealth of directions, admonitions and consolations of the scriptures will be able through God's word to drive out demons and help his brother.'

Life Together

The person who has embraced God's word as truth and life is thereby empowered to speak with authority and to live boldly. That authority never lies within ourselves. It also does not come from simply speaking God's word, but rather from having heard it, believed it and lived it.

THOUGHT: *The person who lives by the word is also empowered by the word.*

Fear of man

'Those who are still afraid of men have no fear of
God and those who have fear of God have ceased to
be afraid of men.'

The Cost of Discipleship

Each one of us has to be our own person. We
need to have a strong sense of what we are
about, set our own direction and live purposefully and boldly. This boldness comes from
knowing that we are living according to God's
intention. In living out God's will, we will be
misunderstood. But we are not to be afraid, for
if we live according to what others want, they
will eventually despise us anyway.

THOUGHT: *If we simply live to please others, we
will be despised; if we live for ourselves, we will be
lost; if we live for God, we will also live for ourselves
and for others.*

Breaking free

'The devil will always be in the place where I ought to have lived and did not wish to live as God's creature in God's world.'

Creation and Fall

When we live from and of ourselves, we will always be in a place where we lack authenticity. In living like that, we will probably lose ourselves to the powerful social forces which seek to dictate to us life's meaning and purpose. When, however, we seek to live as God's creatures in our world, we will always need to free ourselves from these social pressures. For the world's values are not the drumbeat to which we wish to march, for we have heard the voice of another. That voice is not always clear, but it has charmed us into an obedience by faith.

MEDITATION: *To live as God's creatures in our world always means that we have to move from where we are to where God calls us to be.*

A common life

'Christians. . . have common petitions, common thanks, common intercessions to bring to God, and they should do so joyfully and confidently.'

Life Together

Simply to be together in Sunday worship where everything is determined from the front is a sad distortion of what it means to be the church. Life together for Christians is meant to be much more than that. Common prayers, sharing, encouragement, giving, ministry and hospitality are some of the elements of such a life together.

MEDITATION: *If we cannot be the reconciled and serving community, we can hardly proclaim the good news that God is the God of reconciliation and the builder of the new humanity in Christ.*

The spellbinder

'God himself is the skilful one who, by his word of grace, claims and controls our hearts. With the sweet words of his love he attracts us, persuades us, takes charge of our hearts, so that we listen to him as if in a spell and yield to him our obedience.'

Meditating on the Word

If God's word simply adds a bit of information to our knowledge, and if God's love simply adds a bit more warmth and security to our lives, then we are hardly likely to make great changes and commitments in their wake. But where God's word challenges us to the very core of our being and God's love radically transforms us, then great commitments and sacrifices can be expected. God does not charm us with his grace and love so that we will remain mesmerised by his presence, but so that we will serve him freely and boldly in our world.

MEDITATION: *When God casts the spell of his love, it binds us not only to him, but also to his passion for our world.*

Church and state

'The church. . . [must] continually ask the state whether its actions can be justified as legitimate. . .'
No Rusty Swords

Many think that the church should only be concerned about spiritual matters.   But the church is the people of God in the world and, as such, it should be concerned about the whole of life.   This does not mean that the church should tell the government how to conduct its specific affairs.   But it should constantly be challenging the state regarding its priorities and its concerns about freedom, responsibility, justice and its care for the needy.

THOUGHT: *The church which has no social and political concern is a church which simply condones the political status quo.*

Defining the good Christian

'To be a Christian does not mean to be religious in a particular way, to cultivate some particular from of ascetism . . . but to be a man.'

Letters and Papers from Prison

It is always easy to attempt to typify a Christian as a person who has certain religious habits and commitments. Depending on which group the Christian belongs to, this behaviour will be differently defined. Some groups cast spirituality in world-denying terms. Others, rightly, emphasise a world-engaging perspective. But the problem underlying both approaches is that we set up a check list for determining who is a good Christian. Such lists are inevitably too constricting and eventually lead to a narrow legalism. It is doubtful if Jesus himself would make it on some of the spiritual check lists we have created.

MEDITATION: *Out of the central commitment of faith in Jesus Christ, different men and women will work out their commitment in very different ways. In this diversity, they will reflect something of the fullness of Christ.*

Following Christ

'When we are called to follow Christ, we are summoned to an exclusive attachment to his person.'
The Cost of Discipleship

The modern follower of Jesus of Nazareth no longer walks the Galilee road with him. We are to walk many different roads. For some it is the road of politics; for others it is missionary work. Some, in following Christ, embrace a 'secular' career, while others choose a 'spiritual' vocation. All of these are equally important and valid if they spring from the desire to emulate Christ's way of living and doing.

MEDITATION: *The issue is not what road we walk, but who we are following.*

God is already there

'To believe is. . . to find God, his grace and the community of Christ already present.'

Act and Being

When we come to faith, we discover for ourselves what is already true. We certainly don't put God, the Bible or the church on the map. They all have long preceded us. The challenge, however, is that we don't simply conform the God of the church to the God of the Bible and that we don't conform our experience of God simply to that of the church. It is so easy for our new-found faith quickly to become domesticated. While we need to hear the voice of tradition in the life of the church, we also need to hear God's voice anew in the Bible.

THOUGHT: *Each new generation needs to hear God's word anew.*

December

*This is what I mean by worldliness — taking life
in one's stride, with all its duties and problems. . .
It is in such a life that we throw ourselves utterly
into the arms of God and participate
in his sufferings in the world.*

Where world and spirituality meet

'This is what I mean by worldliness — taking life in one's stride, with all its duties and problems. . . It is in such a life that we throw ourselves utterly into the arms of God and participate in his sufferings in the world.'

Letters and Papers from Prison

We are to throw ourselves into all the polyphony of life. As we do so, we also need to throw ourselves into the arms of God. If we simply immerse ourselves in all the challenges of life without the presence and blessing of God, we may well lose ourselves. If, on the other hand, we simply throw ourselves into the arms of God in order to escape the world with its responsibilities, enigmas and challenges, then we may well fool ourselves that we have gained a true form of spirituality.

THOUGHT: *The place where world and spirituality meet is the place where the Christian faces life empowered with the grace and love of God.*

The church of the poor

'The future and the hope for the "bourgeois" church lies in a renewal of its lifeblood, which is only possible if the church succeeds in winning the proletariat.'

Sanctorum Communio

The church of the First World has become the church of the middle classes. The church of the Third World is the church of the poor. The latter is flourishing with new theological creativity and missionary purpose. The former is languishing with its attempts to keep everyone happy on a gospel that knows little of the cost of discipleship. If the church of the rich embraced the cry of the poor and made that its concern, it would itself be saved.

THOUGHT: *We have been preoccupied with saving ourselves and ensuring that the gospel costs nothing. The gospel should cost us everything and, by practising this, we shall be saved.*

Old and new

'It is not necessary that we should discover new ideas in our meditation. It is sufficient if the word, as we read and understand it, penetrates and dwells within us.'

Life Together

Our quiet reflection on a section of scripture may yield astonishingly fresh insights. It more often yields the familiar. This should not be seen as a problem. Our life needs maintenance as much as it should experience bursts of creativity. Hearing God's message again and again may not arouse our excitement, but it may sustain us in the walk of faith.

THOUGHT: *That which we repeatedly think about and embrace as truth will become an integral part of our lives.*

Thankful praise

'To become thankful to God for the sake of Christ and to praise him in the congregation with heart, mouth and hands is what the Psalms wish to teach us.'

Psalms: The Prayer Book of the Bible

We find it difficult to accept that in the final analysis we don't deserve anything. Therefore we might only feel like engaging in celebration, joy and thanksgiving at significant times, or when we receive outstanding gifts. But thanksgiving is always appropriate, particularly when we meet together as the people of God, for there we can thank God for the joy of knowing him and for the very life he gives us.

MEDITATION: *It is the Giver and not the gifts that we need to appreciate.*

The mystery of suffering

'The righteous person knows that God allows him
to suffer so, in order that he may learn to love God
for God's own sake.'

Meditating on the Word

We do not always understand the purpose of
our difficulties and suffering. And usually in
the heat of the moment we find it difficult to
make sense of what is happening to us. We are
blessed if, sometimes in hindsight, we can look
back with understanding and see the purpose
of those hardships. Sometimes, however, we
are not given an understanding of their meaning and are called to link ourselves with the
crucified Jesus who cried, 'My God, why have
you forsaken me?'

MEDITATION: *Suffering is not wasted if it is not
understood. It is only wasted if it hardens our heart
towards the grace and love of God.*

Christ the other

'While I am still reflecting on myself in order to find
Christ, Christ is not there.'

Act and Being

The inward journey to find myself may be a
worthwhile project. But to find myself as the
way to find Christ is doomed to failure. Christ
and my inner self are not one and the same.
This is good news. For it is far better that Christ
be the other, the conversation partner, the One
who stands over against me and yet is for me,
than that he be more of what I am.

MEDITATION: *The distinctions of Creator and creature, of I and thou are there not to divide, but to
complement and to enrich.*

Counsel and help

'God has made it possible for man to seek counsel from others; it would be presumptuous folly on his part not to make use of God's offer.'

Sanctorum Communio

Total self-sufficiency is a myth. And the idea that we only need God's help in our difficulty is a spiritualisation, for we also need to turn to our brothers and sisters for help and encouragement. What constantly must be avoided, however, is that we turn to our friends for help when we should turn to God. What is unequally unhelpful is that we turn to God, but fail to see the helpers that are readily at hand.

PRAYER: *Lord, help me to be open at all times to your guidance and encouragement, and grant that I may be willing to seek out those who can challenge, enrich and help me. Amen.*

My own transformation

'I can no longer condemn or hate a brother for whom I pray, no matter how much trouble he causes me. His face, that hitherto may have been strange and intolerable to me, is transformed in intercession into the countenance of a brother for whom Christ died.'

Life Together

Genuine prayer for the other person cannot but transform my own attitude. It is impossible to commend someone lovingly to the grace of God while maintaining an attitude of bitterness or resentment towards that person. My prayer for the other, first of all, becomes a prayer for myself as I lay down my resentments and seek God's forgiveness and healing.

MEDITATION: *Prayer changes things, particularly the one who prays.*

Devoid of promise

'The work of God cannot be done without due authorisation, otherwise it is devoid of promise.'

The Cost of Discipleship

Sometimes the things we claim that we do for God have nothing to do with him at all. They are merely our own agendas, for we have never stopped long enough to pray and to hear from God. We will soon discover that running with our own agendas is a particularly difficult road to walk, for it is without God's promise, grace and enabling.

MEDITATION: *Work for God should always be done with God.*

Welcoming the past

'The past will come to you once more and be your life's enduring part through thanks and repentance. Feel in the past God's forgiveness and goodness; pray him to keep you today and tomorrow.'

Prayer from Prison

Much of the past simply slips away from us, since forgetfulness is an essential part of our humanity. But in remembering, some of the past returns to us. Sometimes this remembrance calls for thankfulness. At other times it calls for repentance, an appropriate response when we remember things which have never been brought to proper closure.

THOUGHT: *It is not helpful for our present and future conduct if our past is characterised by murky shadows representing issues that have never been properly resolved. For these, we need to seek God's forgiveness in order that our present will not be fed by reactionary impulses.*

Faith and doubt

'A faith which grows doubtful of itself because it considers itself unworthy is a faith which stands in temptation.'

Act and Being

It is not faith that saves us; only God's love in Christ Jesus gives us power to live a new life. Our faith will always be shaky and incomplete. It will always be unworthy. But faith's gaze is not to be on itself, but on him to whom it looks for grace, forgiveness and empowerment.

THOUGHT: *It is not so much a matter of great faith, but faith in a great God.*

Worship God alone

'The law and life are not worthy of adoration, for they are creatures like all others, but the one who is worthy is the Lord of the law and the Lord of the living.'

Creation and Fall

There are those who worship life itself and make much of nature and human creativity or beauty. There are others who magnify human achievement with its laws, ideas, social institutions or scientific technology. The Christian is to appreciate everything thankfully, but to worship God alone. Sadly, Christians often, in worshipping God, appear to reject everything else. This narrow-mindedness has nothing to do with the Bible's vision of life. There we see a love for God leading to a passion for life, beauty, creativity and responsibility.

THOUGHT: *When we acknowledge God as the Creator and Sustainer of our life and world, we can also appreciate all that is good in our world.*

Past acts and present hope

'We pray these Psalms when we regard all that God
does once for his people as done for us.'

Psalms: The Prayer Book of the Bible

We cannot argue that God will act for us in the
same way that he responded to the heart-cry of
the Psalmist. That would be an attempt to
make God predictable. But we can make the
heart-cry of the Psalmist our cry, and believe
that God will respond to us in ways that reflect
his grace and care.

MEDITATION: *God's acts of the past are characterised by grace and great generosity. We can be
confident of nothing less for our own situations.*

Right hearing

'But silence before the word leads to right hearing and thus also to right speaking of the word of God at the right time.'

Life Together

The art of listening has nothing to do with trying to blank out our mind. Instead, it has to do with engaging the other in such a way that what that person has to say can be faithfully heard. Thus right hearing is always a movement from being still to being open and from being open to pressing the other with appropriate questions.

THOUGHT: *Through dialogue with its movement of question and answer, truth can emerge.*

The narrow way

'To confess and testify to the truth as it is in Jesus, and at the same time to love the enemies of that truth... is indeed a narrow way.'

The Cost of Discipleship

The narrow way to which Jesus calls us has nothing to do with narrow-mindedness. Instead, it has everything to do with the tension between tough love and a generous spirit, truth and openness, flexibility and firm commitment, love of God and love for our neighbour, and spirituality and worldly concern. The temptation is always that we opt for one or the other. For example, our pursuit of a firm commitment in our discipleship can so easily lead to rigidity, legalism and narrow-mindedness, rather than a firmness with flexibility marked by grace.

THOUGHT: *When we walk the narrow way, we will seldom please everyone. For the worldly person we will appear to be too spiritual, and for the spiritual person we will probably be regarded as too worldly.*

God as Redeemer and Creator

'It is always the God who has already revealed himself to his people in his word who is said to be known as the Creator of the world.'

Psalms: The Prayer Book of the Bible

From the observation of nature itself, it is unlikely that one comes to faith in the Creator, although nature's spectacular beauty could lead one to praise and adoration. The movement is seldom from nature to the God of the Bible. It is usually the other way round. From the God of scripture, we hear of the Creator who is also our Redeemer. It is our appreciation of God as the Creator which should spur us on to care for our world.

THOUGHT: *Where we only know God as Redeemer and fail to appreciate him as Creator, we may be deflected from part of our task in this world, namely the care of God's earth.*

Preoccupied

'Often we are so burdened and overwhelmed with our thoughts, images and concerns that it may take a long time before God's word has swept all else aside and come through.'

Life Together

We tend to be slavishly preoccupied. Not only do the pressures and concerns of each day crowd in upon us, but we are also constantly living toward the future — planning, hoping, striving for the things we wish to achieve. Consequently, we know little about a centrepoint of stillness where we can hear again those things which God may wish to tell us. We therefore need to take time to become still and lay down all our concerns.

THOUGHT: *Taking time to be still is finally productive time for it revitalises us and provides us with new direction.*

Not our idea of life

'So the Christian lives from the times of God and not
from his own idea of life.'

Temptation

We can live according to our own ideas regarding life's purpose. Frequently, however, these
ideas are simply variations on what our contemporary culture holds up as being important.
These ideas ought to be regarded with grave
suspicion, for their fruit is everywhere to be seen
— self-interest, exploitation, success at any price,
control, progress without due concern for the
quality of life, material security and an ir-
rationality which fails to link actions and consequences. Rather than grasp what lies cheaply
and closely at hand, we need to seek for deeper
answers regarding life's purpose. In the richness of scripture, we can find much by which to
redirect our lives.

THOUGHT: *Life's purpose can never simply lie with
ourselves. Nor does it simply lie in seeking the well-
being of others. Instead, it lies in God who binds us to
our neighbours.*

Our little company as part of the church

'Thus all singing together. . . must serve to widen our spiritual horizon, make us see our little company as a member of the great Christian church on earth.'

Life Together

Whether our church is large or small, it represents only a tiny part of the church on earth. This universal church seethes with diversity. Some of its more radical emphases we may find alienating. But when we all are at prayer, gather at the communion table, sing our praises, bind ourselves to care for each other and enter our world to demonstrate the love and justice of God, then we are indeed one.

THOUGHT: *Radical diversity need never be a problem if we can continue to love each other.*

Good and evil

'The good is for us always only that which has been wrested from evil.'

Creation and Fall

The good always needs to be won. Truth always needs to be discovered. Reality needs to be embraced. Faithfulness requires commitment. The light needs to be sought after. Forgiveness needs to be asked for. Commitment is won through the struggle of working through options. Obedience comes through laying down our lives. Power results from true servanthood. And love constantly needs to be imparted to us. Nothing good simply falls into our lap. Good comes when evil and selfishness are resisted and God's grace and direction is grasped with both hands.

MEDITATION: *The good, which is God's quality of good, is a good that is wonderfully generous and amazingly tough.*

One another

'We speak to one another on the basis of the help we both need. We admonish one another to go the way that Christ bids us to go.'

Life Together

While we like to make distinctions in the Christian community regarding the strong and weak, the mature and the immature, those who are spiritual and those who are less so, the reality is that we are all sinful, lose our way, resist the Spirit, fail in our love towards our brothers and sisters, fail in our commitment to our neighbour, fail to listen to God's direction, rationalise, hide from the truth and neglect some of our responsibilities. Thus we all stand in need of God's grace and forgiveness. And we all need each other's help, encouragement and challenge as we walk the road of following Christ.

PRAYER: *Lord, in my walk of faith help me to realise my limitations, acknowledge my wrongdoing, and seek the encouragement of the least of my brothers and sisters. Amen.*

Knowledge and transformation

'But to be known by God means to become a new man.'

Act and Being

When we truly know God and are known by him, then such knowledge is never formal or theoretical. Rather it is personal, existential and transforming. In other words, we cannot know God and still remain the same. And God's revelation of himself to us is never to leave us where we are, but moves us to adopt a new vision of life. More specifically, God's knowledge of us is never distant. It is personal and practical. It is a knowledge by which he expresses his amazing love for us.

THOUGHT: *To be known by God is to be loved by him, for true knowledge comes only to the one who sees through the eyes of love.*

Illusion or hope

'It's true that the importance of illusion in human life is not to be underestimated, but for the Christian it is essential to have a hope which is based on solid foundations.'

Letters and Papers from Prison

Since we live towards the future, hope is a human characteristic. But there is a world of difference between wishful thinking, illusion or idealism, and Christian hope. Christian hope believes the faithfulness of God and emphasises our human responsibility. It is totally opposed to the idea that we can live the way we like and then trust God to work things out. Instead, Christian hope involves that we act as if everything depended on us and that we pray as if everything depended on God.

MEDITATION: *Only the one who hopes has a future.*

Judge not

'Judging others makes us blind, whereas love is il-
luminating. By judging others, we blind ourselves
to our own evil and to the grace which others are
just as entitled to as we are.'

The Cost of Discipleship

We are not to be gullible; instead, we should
be discerning in our relationships with others.
If someone regularly breaks their word and
acts irresponsibly, then we can hardly continue
to relate to that person as if nothing has hap-
pened. But we cannot withdraw either. Love
calls us to confront, challenge and encourage,
but only in such a way that believes that change
and growth are always possible. Loving confrontation has nothing to do with judging the
other person; instead, it calls both the con-
fronter and the one confronted to grace and
responsibility.

THOUGHT: *We should never put someone in a box
on the basis of past behaviour.*

He came in weakness

'God is weak and powerless in the world, and that is exactly the way, the only way, in which he can be with us and help us.'

Letters and Papers from Prison

The incarnation, God's coming among us in Jesus Christ, has all the trappings of an anti-drama. In many ways it was all so ordinary. And yet it was so very special. But to a large extent it was wonderful only in hindsight. Only a few at the time of his coming really saw and wondered and worshipped. The majority saw nothing very special and finally sided with those who wanted to rid Israel of this Man from Galilee. In this way, God came amongst us in weakness rather than in power, yet in this way alone we could be redeemed.

MEDITATION: *God's weakness will always manifest itself in the power of his grace or his judgment.*

In the presence of his people

'It is the presence of the God of salvation in his congregation for which we give thanks.'

Psalms: The Prayer Book of the Bible

In worship and thanksgiving, we acknowledge God's faithfulness rather than his blessings. God's blessings vary, and he sometimes withholds from us those things that we desire and expect.   But God's faithfulness, steadfastness and trustworthiness can give cause for great rejoicing, even when his blessings and his dealings with us cause us problems.

THOUGHT: *We are truly relying on God's faithfulness when we trust him, not for the peripheral things in our lives, but for those things which are central.*

Freedom and suffering

'Not only action, but also suffering is a way to freedom.'

Letters and Papers from Prison

While we would all prefer a freedom that can be expressed and realised in the world around us, sometimes we are called to possess a freedom within ourselves which cannot as yet be realised in our social structures. Some men and women with a vision for justice have spent years in imprisonment. Freedom for them is not a possession, but a hope. They thus suffer for their freedom in the hope of bringing to birth a freedom that can be practically realised.

THOUGHT: *To embrace freedom may involve embracing suffering, for freedom must always be won from oppression and injustice.*

Judging God's word

'Man is expected to be judge of God's word instead
of simply hearing and doing it.'

Creation and Fall

A passive listening is not the way to hear what
God says. God's word needs to be probed,
pressed for answers and questioned. It needs
to be wrestled with and we need to come to an
understanding as to what is relevant for our
self-understanding and life. If we are aware of
the needs and concerns of our time and read
scripture anew in the light of these concerns,
then we will hear new answers.

THOUGHT: *Part of our task in rightly discerning
God's word to us is to make sure that we do not take
the more convenient parts of scripture and ignore all
that which radically challenges our present lifestyle
and our ecclesiastical structures and traditions.*

The hidden character of the Christian life

'Prayer is the supreme instance of the hidden character of the Christian life. It is the antithesis of self-display. When men pray, they have ceased to know themselves and know only God whom they call upon.'

The Cost of Discipleship

Much in our present-day spirituality is ostentatious and consequently superficial. We are not known for our depth of prayer, inner transformation, integrity and knowledge of God. Not only is it appropriate that we embrace the spiritual disciplines of meditation, prayer and fasting but, more importantly, we need a new vision of the majesty, holiness and power of God.

THOUGHT: *Much of our activism is poor because it is not born out of, or sustained by, an inner spirituality that knows God in the awesomeness of his character and his call upon our lives.*

For what I am responsible

'I am to *rule* over the earth which is and remains my earth, and the more strongly I rule it, the more it is *my* earth.'

Creation and Fall

What I take more or less for granted, I tend not to care too much about either. For real care involves commitment and responsibility. I only care for what I am also responsible. To adopt a strong sense of responsibility for our life and our world should not grow out of a desire for power, possession or control, but from a mandate to care, nurture and responsibly develop all that God has placed within our care.

THOUGHT: *Responsibility and care are dynamically related.*

Promise and fulfilment

'God does not give us everything we want, but he does fulfil his promises.'

Letters and Papers from Prison

Just because we are Christians does not mean that we can automatically grasp and attain God's promises. God's word is never a magical talisman and God's promises are always conditional, for they are applied by God's wisdom. This means that his promises are always realised in his time and in his way. This will always call for faith, perseverance and patience on our part.

THOUGHT: *We often think that God is slow in doing what we ask of him in faith, but his timing is always better than ours.*

APPENDIX

A brief chronology of Bonhoeffer's life

I.

The making of a German theologian

1906	Dietrich Bonhoeffer born in Breslau on February 4
1912	The Bonhoeffer family move to Berlin
1923–24	Two terms' study at the University of Tübingen
1923	Three months' travel in Rome and North Africa
	Beginning of study in Berlin
1927	*Sanctorum Communio* accepted for doctorate (published 1930, English translation 1963)
1928	First theological examination in Berlin
1928–29	Assistant pastor in Barcelona

1929–30	Assistant pastor in Berlin
1930	*Act and Being* accepted as lectureship qualification at Berlin University (published 1931, English translation 1962)
1930–31	'Sloane Fellow' at Union Theological Seminary, New York
1931	Returns to Germany

II.

The beginning of the church struggle

1931	Entry into the ecumenical movement
	September: appointed youth secretary at Cambridge University
	October: chaplain to Technical High School, Berlin
	November: ordination
	Began difficult confirmation class in working-class suburb
1932	April: attends the youth commission in London and disarmament conference in Geneva

Nazis gain 230 seats in German parliament

July: ecumenical conference in eastern Europe

First draft of *Schöpfung und Sünde* (English translation *Creation and Fall*, 1961)

Dr Bell, Bishop of Chichester, becomes president of World Council for Life and Work

Karl Bath's *Church Dogmatics* begins to appear

November: 'German Christians' win one-third of seats in Church of Old Prussian Union

1933   30 January: Adolf Hitler becomes Chancellor of Germany

February 1: interrupted broadcast by Dietrich Bonhoeffer, where he attacked the 'leadership principle'

July 23: general church election. 'German Christians' gain seventy per cent of votes

September 27: Ludwig Muller becomes national bishop

III.

A leader in the Confessing Church

1933	April 7: the Aryan Clauses forbid those of Jewish origin holding office in the state church
	Bonhoeffer deals at once with the Jewish question
	June 25: Karl Barth issues No. 1 of 'Theological Existence Today', dealing with the effect of the Aryan Clauses on the church
	September 7: Bonhoeffer works with Niemöller in the preparation of the Pastors' Emergency League
	October: leave of absence to become pastor of two German-speaking congregations in London
	November 27–30: Bradford conference of German pastors in England
1934	January 25: Hitler receives the leaders of the German evangelical churches

	May 29 and 31: the first synod of the Confessing Church at Barmen
	August: World Alliance Universal Christian Council conference at Fano in Denmark.
1935	Plans to visit India
	Call to leadership of a theological college for the Confessing Church
	April 26: students met for their first class with Bonhoeffer at Zingst on the Baltic
	June 24: theological college moved to Finkenwalde
	Bonhoeffer writes 'The Confessing Church and the Ecumenical Movement' at Finkenwalde

IV.

The training of the Confessing Church

1935	June: work commences at Finken-walde
	November: first five circular letters
1936	February: fourth synod of the Confessing Church at Bad Oeynhausen

— protest from Finkenwalde

February–March: tour of Denmark and Sweden with his students

March 14: sermon on Judas preached at Finkenwalde

August: Olympic Games in Berlin

August 20–26: Universal Council for Life and Work meets at Chamby with two German delegations

September: Finkenwalde closed by order of Himmler

Publication of *The Cost of Discipleship*

V.

The years of decision

1937   July 1: the arrest of Martin Nie-möller

July 12–26: ecumenical conference on 'Church, Community and State' meets at Oxford without a German delegation

November: twenty-seven of the men from Finkenwalde arrested

1938	February: Bonhoeffer's first contact with Sack, Oster, Canaris and Beck, the leaders of the political resistance
	March 12: Hitler annexes Austria
	June 20: Finkenwalde reunion at Zingst — Bible study on *Temptation* published posthumously
	September: *Life Together* written at Göttingen
	October 1: Hitler annexes Sudentenland
	November 9: 'The Crystal Night'
1939	March and April: Bonhoeffer in London with Bell, Niebuhr, Leibholz and Visser't Hooft
	March 15: Hitler annexes the rest of Czechoslovakia
	June 4: Bonhoeffer's departure for London and then the USA
	June 15: arrival in the USA
	July 1: Britain declares that she cannot tolerate further territorial demands by Hitler
	July 27: Bonhoeffer's arrival back in Berlin

August 25: Bonhoeffer made an agent of the *Abwehr*, thereby avoiding conscription

September 1: Hitler invades Poland

September 3: Britain and France declare war on Germany

VI.

The period of political resistance

1940	March 17: the Gestapo break up the seminary efforts in Doslin and Gross-Schölnwitz
	Begins work on *Ethics*
1941	February 24: visits Karl Barth in Switzerland on an *Abwehr* assignment
	October: introduced into the inner resistance circle of the *Abwehr* and made a key resistance figure
1942	May 30: flies to Stockholm to meet Bishop Bell to confer about Allied reaction to a possible political overthrow

September: an *Abwehr* agent apprehended for attempting to smuggle currency over the border; his comments lead to evidence incriminating both von Dohnanyi and Bonhoeffer

1943   April 5: von Dohnanyi and Bonhoeffer arrested; Bonhoeffer sent to the military prison, Tegel, in Berlin
July: intensive and continuous interrogations

1944   June 6: the Normandy landing
July 20: the assassination attempt on Hitler by Count von Stauffenberg
October 8: Bonhoeffer removed from Tegel and sent to the high security prison, Prinz-Albrecht-Strasse
Writings ceased

1945   February: Bonhoeffer shipped to Buchenwald
April 3: begins the final trip from Buchenwald
April 9: arrives at Flossenburg; hanged alongside Oster, Sack and Canaris — the last day of World War II

BIBLIOGRAPHY

I.

Primary sources

BONHOEFFER, Dietrich, *Letters & Papers from Prison* (translated from the German *Widerstand und Ergebung: Briefe und Aufzeichnungen aus der Haft*), Collins, London, 1953 and 1971

BONHOEFFER, Dietrich, *Life Together* (translated from the German *Gemeinsames Leben*), SCM, London, 1954

BONHOEFFER, Dietrich, *Ethics* (translated from the German *Ethik*), SCM, London, 1955

BONHOEFFER, Dietrich, *Temptation* (translated from the German *Versuchung*), Macmillan, New York, 1955

BONHOEFFER, Dietrich, *Act and Being* (translated from the German *Akt und Sein*), Harper and Row, New York, 1956

BONHOEFFER, Dietrich, *The Cost of Discipleship* (translated from the German *Nachfolge*), SCM, London, 1959

BONHOEFFER, Dietrich, *Creation and Fall: A Theological Interpretation of Genesis 1–3* (translated from the German *Schöpfung und Sünde*), Macmillan, New York, 1959

BONHOEFFER, Dietrich, *Sanctorum Communio*, Collins, London, 1963

BONHOEFFER, Dietrich, *No Rusty Swords: Letters, Lectures and Notes 1928–1936* (translated from Bonhoeffer's *Gesammelte Schriften*, Vols. 1–4), Collins, London, 1965

BONHOEFFER, Dietrich, *The Way to Freedom: Letters, Lectures and Notes 1935–1939* (translated from *Gesammelte Schriften*, Vols. 1–4), Collins, London, 1966

BONHOEFFER, Dietrich, *Christology* (translated from Bonhoeffer's *Gesammelte Schriften*, Vol. 3), Collins, London, 1966

BONHOEFFER, Dietrich, *Psalms: The Prayer Book of the Bible* (translated from the German *Das Gebetbuch der Bibel*), Augsburg, Minneapolis, 1970

BONHOEFFER, Dietrich, *Prayer from Prison, Prayers and Poems* (translated from the German *Von Guten Mächten: Gebete und Gedichte, interpretiert von Johann Christoph Hampe*), Collins, London, 1977

BONHOEFFER, Dietrich, *Fiction from Prison: Gathering up the Past* (translated from the German *Fragmente aus Tegel: Drama und Roman*), Fortress, Philadelphia, 1981

BONHOEFFER, Dietrich, *Meditating on the Word* (translated from selections of *Gesammelte Schriften*), Cowley, Cambridge, MA., 1986

II.

Secondary sources, Bonhoeffer biographies

BETHGE, E., *Dietrich Bonhoeffer: Theologian, Christian, Contemporary*, Collins, London, 1970

BOSANQUET, Mary, *The Life and Death of Dietrich Bonhoeffer*, Hodder and Stoughton, London, 1968

GILL, Theodore A., *Memo for a Movie: A Short Life of Dietrich Bonhoeffer*, SCM, London, 1971

MARLÉ, René, *Bonhoeffer: The Man and His Work*, Geoffrey Chapman, London, 1968

ROBERTSON, Edwin, *The Shame and the Sacrifice: The Life and Teaching of Dietrich Bonhoeffer*, Hodder and Stoughton, London, 1987

ZIMMERMAN, W. and SMITH, R.G. (eds), *I Knew Dietrich Bonhoeffer*, Collins, London, 1966

III.

Secondary sources, theological and ethical works

BURTNESS, James H., *Shaping the Future: The Ethics of Dietrich Bonhoeffer*, Fortress, Philadelphia, 1985

DAY, Thomas I., *Dietrich Bonhoeffer on Christian Community and Common Sense*, Edwin Mellen, New York, 1982

DE GRUCHY, John, *Dietrich Bonhoeffer: Witness to Jesus Christ*, Collins, London, 1988

DUMAS, André, *Dietrich Bonhoeffer: Theologian of Reality*, SCM, London, 1971

FEIL, Ernst, *The Theology of Dietrich Bonhoeffer*, Fortress, Philadelphia, 1985

GODSEY, J.D., *The Theology of Dietrich Bonhoeffer*, SCM, London, 1960

GODSEY, J.D. and KELLY, G.B. (eds), *Ethical Responsibility: Bonhoeffer's Legacy to the Churches*, Edwin Mellen, New York, 1981

HOPPER, David, H., *A Dissent on Bonhoeffer*, Westminster, Philadelphia, 1975

KUHNS, W., *In Pursuit of Dietrich Bonhoeffer*, Burns and Oates, London, 1967

MARTY, M.E. (ed.), *The Place of Bonhoeffer*, SCM, London, 1963

OTT, Heinrich, *Reality and Faith: The Theological Legacy of Dietrich Bonhoeffer*, Lutterworth, London, 1971

PHILLIPS, J.A., *The Form of Christ in the World: A Study of Bonhoeffer's Christology*, Collins, London, 1967

RASMUSSEN, Larry, *Dietrich Bonhoeffer: His Significance for North Americans*, Fortress, Minneapolis, 1990

ROBERTSON, Edwin, *Bonhoeffer Heritage,* Hodder and Stoughton, London, 1989

WOELFEL, J.W., *Bonhoeffer's Theology: Classical and Revolutionary*, Abingdon, Nashville, 1970